# THE
# PURSUIT

## REFRAMING PURITY
## AS A RELATIONSHIP,
## NOT AN ACCOMPLISHMENT

JOSH LIVINGSTON & DAN MARTIN

# WHAT PEOPLE ARE SAYING ABOUT *THE PURSUIT*

"It's frustrating when something meant to do so much good ends up doing so much harm. But that's exactly what the evangelical 'sexual purity movement' did to so many young people who embraced it. It was a noble idea that unfortunately launched from a flawed assumption that unwittingly aimed everyone in the wrong direction. Fortunately, there's a powerful solution that doesn't abandon that noble idea. Livingston and Martin have captured it all in this new book. Frankly, this book should now become required reading of any person, parent, or pastor that wants to set the people they love up to enjoy God's gift of sex the way it was intended to be enjoyed. It's a book that offers genuine hope. Pure hope."

**DR. TIM KIMMEL**
Founder of Grace Based Families
& Author of *Grace Based Parenting*

"For far too long, the Church was relatively silent around the topic of sex. In more recent decades, voices have begun to rise up, but many have taken strange forms—either centering around rule lists and shame-mongering or allowing culture to lead the sexual narrative and piecing scriptures around world views in order to justify man's desires and remain relevant to a confused society. The Pursuit does a beautiful and effective job of inviting you to step back and zoom out. To see the greater narrative of God's story and how sex—in its right-natured and God-honoring form—was actually designed to serve as a proclamation of His Good News! But in order to walk in this beautiful truth, our hearts must first be captivated by the purity of His love for us and drawn into a relationship with One who is pure. The Pursuit holds the key to your healing, your renewed understanding, and your hope in the days to come!"

**MO ISOM AIKEN**

*New York Times* bestselling author of
*Sex, Jesus, and the Conversations the Church Forgot*
& Founder of BOLDLIFE INITIATIVE

"The Pursuit provides a refreshing yet biblical approach to the concept of sexual purity. In a culture where purity is merely defined as something achieved by sheer will power, Josh and Dan provide a better understanding of what it means to embrace purity as God intended."

**ALLEN PARR**

Th. M Dallas Theological Seminary
Founder of "The Beat" & YouTube Influencer

Fedd Books
P.O. Box 341973
Austin, TX 78734
www.thefeddagency.com

Published in association with The Fedd Agency, Inc., a literary agency.
Unless otherwise noted, all scripture quotations are taken from THE HOLY BIBLE,

NEW INTERNATIONAL VERSION®, NIV® Copyright © 1973, 1978, 1984, 2011 by Biblica, Inc.® Used by permission. All rights reserved worldwide.

Scripture marked NKJV was taken from the New King James Version®. Copyright © 1982 by Thomas Nelson. Used by permission. All rights reserved.

ISBN: 978-1-949784-70-1
eISBN: 978-1-949784-71-8

Library of Congress Number: 2021908996

Printed in the United States of America

Cover: Deryn Pieterse

To the men and women who have come before us in our attempt to tell God's beautiful story of sex and what it really means to pursue purity.

Thank you for paving the way so we could bring the message of pureHOPE to a people hungry for a better narrative.

May this book impact many around the world and most importantly, honor our Lord and Savior, Jesus Christ.

# CONTENTS

# INTRODUCTION

## IMAGINE A WORLD FREE . . .

Chances are, if you've grown up in the church, you're already suspicious of this book. First line of the introduction, and you already don't trust us. And we get it. You've been here before. You've read tons of books on purity. You've heard tons of sermons. You know the score here, and you're not about to be fooled again into reading yet another book that pounds you over the head with messages of shame and fear. But, friend, I hope you'll stick around because the journey we're about to embark on together isn't like the other books and sermons on purity that you've encountered.

We're not here to tell you what music to listen to, what shows to watch, or how to dress. We're here to appeal to your heart, soul, and mind, and to walk with you as we explore the narrative of sexuality and to recapture the beauty, sacredness, and life-giving attributes it brings. We believe that when we better understand this narrative, it leads us to live differently. Not because we've unlocked some magical strategy or figured out a creative, new method of self-restraint, but rather, an understanding of the sacredness and beauty of sexuality and what a gift it is. Once we understand what we're truly dealing with when it comes to sexuality, that knowledge and understanding naturally changes how we live.

Still not sure you can trust this book? You've probably heard other authors or pastors say that they've uncovered some new way to view purity that will change your life. But honestly, our approach to understanding purity and sexuality isn't new. Everything we're going to talk about in the pages that follow comes straight from Scripture. The thing is, the "purity culture" and our secular culture's view of sexuality have seriously distorted the way we talk about purity, sex, and relationships in both secular and sacred spaces. So while the narrative of sexuality we're about to explain to you isn't new, it will probably feel new because it's pretty different from what any of us were taught in our churches, purity balls, or rallies where we all pledged to save sex for marriage.

Also, we're not here to talk to you in frustrating, weird, upsetting, or cringe-worthy analogies. We're not going to use vague, confusing terms such as "giving your heart away," and we promise not to depict your wedding with the people you "gave your heart to," joining you and your future spouse at the altar. Men, we're not going to talk about sexuality within purity using military analogies, and there will be no hunter/gatherer references here. We're not going to summon your "warrior within." And, women, we're not going to liken you to a rose, a gum, a shoe, or a cake. We'll also not be talking about fairy tales, princes, frogs, or princesses. Men, we're not here to talk about what a slave you are to lust and offer ways to white knuckle your way through life as this pitiful, sex-charged monster. And, women, we're not here to heap the responsibility of a man's purity on you by telling you what to wear (or not) or how to "behave properly" around men.

Did you just relax a little bit? We hope so, because we've got some amazing stuff to talk about. There are some myths, misconceptions, and outright lies about sex, sexuality, and purity that we're going to unravel. We'd like to invite you—no, implore you—to give us a shot here. Read this book in its entirety, because we're here to offer you hope and freedom from any shame you've been taught in your past. Better yet, we're here to show you the amazing plans and intentions God has when it comes to sex and sexuality. I want you to hear the grace, the healing, and the freedom Christ offers us when we truly understand His narrative for sexuality. Because once we understand God's intention for sex and the narrative He is weaving through sexuality, we can be a better steward of our sexuality rather than feeling like a slave to it. And most importantly, when we understand more of what God intends for our lives and what He wants to show us and teach us through sex, we can better understand our Savior and grow even closer to Him.

In short, when we understand God's better story of sex and live it out in our lives, we start to experience freedom.

At this point, you may be wondering who "we" are. We are pureHOPE, and our vision is a world free of sexual brokenness. By pointing people to God's truth and helping them understand God's story of sex, they can begin to live a life rooted in these four tenets: Prayer, Understanding, Resolve, and Engagement.

That's why we (Josh and Dan) are writing this book together. We want to inspire hope, breathe new life, shine light on God's forgiving power, and testify to Jesus' love for you! We certainly haven't written this book on our own. Our entire pureHOPE team has been involved, and we have collaborated in hopes that you can walk in freedom today. Thanks for joining us on this journey!

---

Now, look around you. More and more, if feels as though the world is in incredibly dark times. Our communities are in turmoil and there is sin, sickness, and death all around us. The prince of darkness is hard at work, twisting truth into lies at every turn. It's something we see happening in both secular and sacred spaces, and it's turning us into a highly sexualized, highly broken society.

- The divorce rate among the Christian community is the same as the greater population, and one of the leading causes of divorce is infidelity or sexual brokenness of some kind.[1]
- Sixty-two percent of teens and young adults have received a text, email, or direct message with a sexually explicit image.[2]
- Most kids are exposed to pornography by age eleven and see over fourteen thousand sexualized messages a year.[3]
- The United Nations says that two million children alone are prostituted in commercial sex trade.[4]

And the bleak statistics chronicling the sexual brokenness of our world only stack up from there. Looking at facts such as these, observing the dissolution of relationships and marriages of those around you (or perhaps even your own), and hearing the stories of those raised in the church who have serious wounds at the hands of harmful, incorrect teachings about sexuality and purity, or those who have faced abuse from trusted leaders in the church feeds the feeling that there is no place free from this kind of darkness.

But what if we told you it doesn't have to be this way? What if we told you that the chaos and pain we see around us is so far from the story God intended to tell? It's true! God's intention for purity, God's intention for sex is something far more meaningful, far more powerful, and far more beautiful than anything we've been taught before. And better yet, when

we can step into the truth of God's better story of sex and truly understand what purity is all about, we can begin stepping away from the sexual
brokenness of the world and step toward a loving Father who forgives and
makes all things new.

That's where we are heading in this book. In Part One, we will look
at purity culture and reevaluate God's design for purity. After that, we'll
talk about sex. The world throws its understanding of sex at us every day,
so in Part Two, we'll dive even further into Scripture and explore God's
much better story of sex. Finally, in Part Three, we'll get practical and talk
about how our past doesn't define us and that we can walk into our future
in freedom.

So what do you say? Are you ready to begin the journey?

# PART ONE

# GOD'S DESIGN FOR PURITY

# CHAPTER 1

# YOU CAN'T SAVE YOURSELF

## JOSH

It is difficult to count the ways the Lord has blessed my life. One of the greatest blessings was growing up in a home that put the Lord first. If you ever came by our house, one of the first things you would see in a small picture frame was "As for me and my house, we will serve the Lord" (Joshua 24:15, NKJV). Even though the address has changed, every time I go to my parents' house, that same verse still hangs on the wall and is still very much the core of our family.

What did that mean for me growing up? My entire family was involved in the church—it was more or less a second home for us. Whether I wanted to or not, we went to church. Even though it may have felt obligatory at times, I am grateful for the foundation because, from a very early age, I felt God's hand on me and I wanted live for Him. If I'm being honest, I loved Jesus, but it wasn't my relationship with Him that developed as much

3

as it was my relationship with the church and the friends, activities, and events therein. I trusted the authority of those in leadership positions. If our pastor or youth leader said it, I trusted it as gospel truth and didn't rightly divide the scriptures.

I remember hearing the word "purity" come up a lot, but it was always with the caveat that I had to work hard to obtain it. I knew abstaining from sex until marriage was biblical, but I didn't really understand God's design and felt as if I had to play by a difficult set of rules. My idea of purity was fear-driven because I didn't want to mess up or disappoint anyone, let alone God.

Honestly, playing multiple sports in high school and then playing college baseball was enough of a distraction that I wasn't always thinking about girls. Baseball was my life, so I may not have had the healthiest relationship with Jesus, but when opportunities arose that I knew would lead me down the wrong path, I fled. I'm so grateful that my wife is the only woman I've ever slept with, *but* hear this: I am *not* any more pure than you are! Whatever actions your past might hold, God wants to tell His story through you, so you can receive His forgiveness and grace that purifies.

What do I mean by that? When Jesus came to Earth, He came to tell a beautiful story, a story far better than anything we've ever heard or experienced before. Christ and His sacrifice on the cross introduced incredibly important and life-changing perspectives into the world: a personal relationship with God, repentance, and renewal. Thanks to Jesus paying for our sins on the cross, we can now walk daily with God and receive renewed grace and love each and every day. Once we choose to accept and follow Jesus, we find ourselves free—free from shame, free from fear, and free from our past.

God's story is one of hope and renewal and second chances. It's one that defies expectations, and it is more wonderful than we could ever imagine. Yes, we serve a God of forgiveness and restoration, something that we saw when He sent His only Son to die on the cross for our sins, but this forgiveness and restoration is a story that God tells us every day if we're willing to listen. Creation is singing God's story, and we only have to open our eyes to see the beauty of His plans as they play out around us.

Yet, despite this amazing story of love, forgiveness, freedom, and peace that Jesus came to Earth to tell, when it comes to sex and purity, we tend to distort that part of the story. We've always known that secular spaces have a different perspective and rulebook when it comes to sex, but it can feel a bit more surprising that within the church, we've managed to lose the plot of God's story of and intention for sex when He calls us to live a life of purity.

Perhaps that's your story. Maybe you've struggled with the way Christians and the church as a whole discuss sex and purity. Purity culture, as it's come to be known, pounded into our heads for years that the idea of "purity" was an achievement to unlock and a goal we could achieve on our own. More specifically, according to purity culture, the pursuit of purity was taught as though its ultimate goal was to get you to your wedding night a virgin, and that once you reached that goal, you could check "maintain your purity" off your list.

While the idea that purity means saving sex for marriage might seem like a simple and straightforward idea, in practice it can turn the entire pursuit of purity into a vapid, meaningless, and outdated pursuit. Anyone who was once a hormonal teenager can tell you that this white-knuckle grip on so-called purity really ends up morphing into a search for loopholes where we can have fun but still hang on to our purity. And if we spend our days focusing on how we can bargain our way into keeping ourselves pure with caveats such as "we can do *this*, we just can't do *that*," we cheapen God's call to purity and His story of sex. If we're focused solely on how much we can get away with over what God is truly calling us to, purity becomes a pass/fail test that sends many of us struggling to connect on a more intimate level with someone we're dating. We are left to suffocate under shame if we "give anything away," or feel left out of the conversation entirely.

By its own verbiage, purity becomes quite problematic pretty quickly. Think about the most common phrase used by Christ followers when they explain their decision to remain obedient to God's way in their romantic relationships. They say, "I'm saving myself for marriage." Where in the rest of Jesus' teachings are we called to save ourselves from anything? Where are we told that it is by our own volition that we do anything? The problem with how we've explained purity in the church is how much of the emphasis we've put on our own effort, when the very act of becoming a Christ follower is falling at the feet of Jesus, admitting our own shortcomings, admitting that we cannot do anything on our own, and inviting Jesus to guide our lives.

So it's not surprising that so many of us have found the act of "saving ourselves" too tough a task. Some describe having sex before marriage as *losing* your virginity or *losing* your purity (making purity and virginity into synonyms is already misleading), which turns purity into something we can keep hold of or lose ourselves. And for some, protecting purity has prove to be too steep a challenge. Maybe we "lost" our purity to someone we dated for a long time, or maybe it came in a night where we got too caught up in the moment. Or, tragically, maybe our purity was taken from us by someone forcefully. Either way, purity culture tells us that we've failed. We couldn't manage to save ourselves, so while Jesus can come in and forgive us, we are ultimately damaged goods. We've all likely heard the stories of object lessons used by youth groups to describe what happens when a person has sex before marriage, comparing the person to a piece of chewed up gum or a rose that has been touched and bruised and broken.

Christ followers are promised a life of grace, love, and forgiveness, but for some reason it was decided that when it came to purity and sex, none of that applied. The narrative of redemption—the story of Jesus' amazing love for us and the daily renewal we receive in Him—somehow got wildly distorted, turning sex and purity into something we must achieve on our own, and if we don't, we've ruined everything. We've *lost*.

Conversely, many of us were also taught that if we did manage to "save ourselves" for our future spouse, it meant that we were in for a life of sexual pleasure. Starting on that very first night after the wedding, we'd magically flip a switch in our brains, be ready to have sex, be knowledgeable and good at it, and everything would be perfect in the bedroom always and forever. But that hasn't been a lot of our stories either. Some of us had trouble flipping that switch, finally releasing all of those urges and desires we spent years working *so hard* to suppress. Some of us had trouble physically connecting with our new spouse. Some of us had trouble articulating our feelings and needs with our spouse, and it made sex a point of tension in the marriage. Some of us suddenly felt very trapped by the idea of spending the rest of our lives with that one person forever. Finding yourself on your wedding night struggling with sex instead of enjoying it has left many feeling cheated and lied to, wondering, *If everything was about achieving purity, why are things so hard now that I'm here? Is this what winning is supposed to feel like?*

Just as the idea of saving ourselves is about as far from Christ's message as anything can be, so is the idea of reaching a Christian milestone and finally having a perfect, conflict-free life. Jesus never promised us a life free from trouble—in fact He often tells His followers that living His way can increase trouble in this life. However, He always promised to be with us, and that through the hardship He would help us and it would all be worth it. Why would Jesus warn us of this in every aspect of our lives as believers but make sex the one exception? In short, He wouldn't.

So why have we allowed this lie to permeate our churches and our homes? Why have we decided that when we talk about sex and purity, we'll ignore Jesus' teachings and turn them into accomplishments we achieve on our own? Why do we believe that failing will destroy us, and that once we reach the finish line of purity, the rest of our married life will be perfect? Unfortunately, this teaching that sometimes comes straight from God's very own people has sold His plan wildly short. Purity is about so much more than waiting until you're married to have sex. Purity is so much more than a test we can pass or fail, and just like everything in God's story and everything else God calls us to, purity isn't something we can mess up so badly that we become a lost cause forever.

In short, the church has had a problem with how to approach purity. The first step to understanding God's better story for sex is reframing how we talk about purity. Purity is not something we obtain from our good behavior—purity is a relationship.

# CHAPTER TWO

# PURITY IS
# A RELATIONSHIP

## DAN

God has written a beautiful story for our lives—and part of that story includes sex. God's story of sex has an intentional design, and not just for the years before we get married. Better still, God's story of sex doesn't end on your wedding night. It also doesn't exclude you if you're single, if you get married later in life, if you've lost a spouse, or if you've gone through a divorce. Why? Because His call for us to pursue purity is far better than a frenetic race to the altar, and it reaches far beyond the act of having sex with another person. God has given us sex as a gift, and it's a part of the amazing story He reveals to us each day we follow after Him. Jesus calls us to live a life of purity in pursuit of Him, not in the pursuit of a status or title. He is the end of our story—the ultimate prize—and by declaring "It is finished" on the cross, He has ensured that we'll make it to the eternal end. The pursuit of purity is the pursuit of Jesus, who makes us pure. It means the reward of eternity with Him, and that goes far beyond losing our virginity on our wedding night because we "kept ourselves pure."

As followers of Jesus, one of the foundational pieces of our worldview is that we cannot remain pure on our own. We need Jesus in this lifelong pursuit of purity. God created the journey, and the boundaries (or guardrails as we call them) He sets for us are there to keep us on track and protect us, not fill us with fear and shame. His commands are for our own good. If purity is something we must obtain on our own, it can make the idea of bumping into one of those guardrails (or driving right through it) feel terrifying. And if we do, we've fallen off the track, so we're done, right? Wrong! If we are pursuing Jesus, He is renewing and purifying us daily. And when we realize the truth of God's better story of sex, purity becomes something Jesus does in us rather than something we do for ourselves. So even in those moments when we veer off track or burst through the guardrails that Jesus has put in place to protect us, we aren't lost. Jesus is there to pick us up and continue purifying us.

God's story of sex is so much better than anything the world and anything purity culture teaches us. His call for us to pursue purity is one that is meant to push us to make the choice every day to continue following Jesus and allowing Him to do His redemptive work in our hearts. And even better, God's story of sex is meant to reveal Himself and His plan for His kingdom.

So it doesn't matter what your history is, and it doesn't matter where you are in your life. The great news is, Jesus is telling a beautiful story in your life, and He is calling you to pursue Him daily as He works to grow you and purify you. Purity is important. We serve a holy God, and we are all sinners. But we've shifted the focus of purity to rest largely on virginity, and by focusing on that one area, we've missed the giant, beautiful tapestry that Christ is weaving for us in our relationship with Him and His better story of sex. It's so much better than anything we've been told before, and just like every other part of a relationship with Jesus, there is so much more grace and love than we could have ever dreamed.

It's time to reframe the discussion of purity and take a new look at what God intended for us, His children created in His image. Purity was never meant to be a fight you endured on your own to reach an arbitrary goal, but a pursuit of Jesus in a story God has already written. As Christ followers, it's a journey we're promised to complete, and one that we'll never embark on alone. And honestly, if we looked at purity as a person—as a relationship and a journey we were going to finish successfully rather than a pass/fail test we have to conquer on our own strength—how much more freely would we move through life and move closer to Jesus?

This is the good news we have got for you. Just like, well, everything in this life, Jesus' plan and His story are so much better than anything we could imagine. God's story of sex is one that is life-changing and life-giving, so we've got to reframe our understanding when it comes to purity.

## A PURE LIFE

If purity isn't about virginity but about a relationship, what does that actually mean in practice? In short, if purity is about relationship, it means we must reframe our entire focus when it comes to how we *pursue* purity. Purity as a relationship means that we are no longer pursuing a box we can check, we aren't fighting to achieve a goal, and we certainly aren't working under the rules of a pass/fail test. Recognizing purity as a relationship means we can understand the pursuit of purity as the pursuit of Jesus and deepening our relationship with Him. This perspective of purity comes straight from the Bible. In 1 John 3:3 it says, "All who have this hope in him purify themselves, just as he is pure."

Think about our life as Christ followers. We aren't working to become perfect and sinless. In fact, the entire point of God sending His one and only Son is for every one of us to realize we are lost without Jesus. We must realize we cannot save ourselves and acknowledge that we need to accept Jesus' salvation. And while we work each day to get closer to God and become more like Him, we know we won't ever become perfect on this side of heaven. We know that Jesus will spend each day working in our hearts and growing us to be more like Him; but our ultimate goal is that when we get to the end of this life, we get to stand before God and hear Him say to us, "Well done, good and faithful servant!" (Matthew 25:21) as we embark on spending an eternity with Him.

Purity is a vital piece of that puzzle to knowing God and becoming more like Him. Just as Jesus spends each day working in our hearts healing, renewing, guiding, and blessing, He spends each day purifying us. We're not doing anything to become pure and our actions don't make us more or less pure, rather it is Christ's work in us that makes us pure. And He does this work in all areas of our lives—not just our sexuality.

The Bible talks a great deal about purity through the salvation we receive in Jesus. In Romans 3:23–26 it says,

> For all have sinned and fall short of the glory of God,
> and all are justified freely by his grace through the
> redemption of Christ Jesus. God presented Christ
> as a sacrifice of atonement, through the shedding

of his blood—to be received by faith. He did this
to demonstrate his righteousness, because in his
forbearance he had left the sins committed before-
hand unpunished—he did it to demonstrate his
righteousness at the present time, so as to be just and
the one who justifies those who have faith in Jesus.

And circling back to the verse we mentioned earlier, 1 John 3:3, we
see that our relationship and pursuit of Jesus purifies us because Jesus
Himself is pure.

So what are the Scriptures saying here? In short, they're saying that
Jesus paid the price for us. His sacrifice on the cross covered our sins, and
we have been made new in Him. That salvation and freedom from sin are
available to anyone who accepts Christ into their hearts. But the thing
about having an intimate relationship with someone who is holiness and
purity incarnate is that we too must become holy and pure. And as it says
in I John, all of us who have hope from our salvation in Jesus will also be
made pure in Him. No one is too broken for Jesus to fix, and our purity
comes from work that Jesus has already done on the cross. As Christ followers, we get to rely fully on that work on the cross, and rest assured that
we can trust fully in Him and the work He is doing in us rather than our
accomplishments or failures.

This is a massive change from what many of us were told from fear and
shame-based teaching on purity. I remember sharing this concept during
a talk at a church in Dallas. I had just kicked off the event by introduc-
ing pureHOPE, then started talking about reframing the way we think of
purity from an accomplishment to a relationship. I explained to the audience that purity isn't something we can win or lose by our behavior, but

rather something we gain from a relationship with the One who is purifying us. Suddenly, a middle-aged man stood up and asked if he could say something. He simply stated, "You are speaking life into me right now! I have never heard this before, and I just have to say thank you!" That man's statement expressed how transformative it can be when we properly understand the truth of purity. In two sentences, he managed to show the whole room the freedom and life we can find when we realize that purity is a person—Jesus—and we can let go of the baggage we feel as we try and fail to "save ourselves." Purity is a relationship rather than an accomplishment. Jesus did the work, and we need only to follow Him.

It's a very different message than most of us grew up hearing, but the Scriptures shed light on an important truth: purity isn't the same thing as virginity. Not only that, the pursuit of purity comes from having a relationship with Jesus Christ, not the pursuit of virginity. Our purity comes from the work Jesus did on the cross and the work He continues to do in you and me, and it suddenly takes the pressure and the fear and the shame away from how you and I conduct our everyday lives. Because of this truth, we no longer have to race to our wedding night or rationalize about how far is too far, because purity isn't in our hands, and purity is so much more than whether or not we're having sex. We're meant to live our lives in pursuit of Jesus—it's up to us to follow after Him while He makes us new each day. Suddenly, that turns something that might have felt very restrictive or vapid into a meaningful, life-giving pursuit. It also means that those who have given up on the race to "save themselves" for marriage, feeling it was too hard to guard their own purity, haven't actually lost anything. And better yet, those who might have abandoned the purity culture lifestyle and swung to the other end of the extreme of "if it feels good, do it," can find new purpose and meaning when they reframe their understanding of purity. In order to understand this new view of purity, we first have to understand who God created us to be—we have to realize we are created in the very image of God!

## IMAGE-BEARERS

The freedom we can find in reframing conversations of purity can be utterly life-giving, but it is important to remember that just because we serve a God of grace and second chances, it doesn't mean we can live without rules. Any good king, any good parent, and even a good temporary caretaker understands that rules, boundaries, and guardrails are put in place to keep everyone safe and healthy. And it's the very same thing when it comes to sex.

When we choose to follow Jesus, our past, present, and future sins are covered in His blood. Still, we are called daily to step away from our life of sin to become more like Christ. This command doesn't stop with our sexuality, and it's why it is vital we reframe our understanding of purity to be more than a synonym for virginity. Just as Christ uses our lives to tell amazing stories of redemption, perfect love, and creating beauty from ashes, He's doing the same thing when it comes to sex. And that story is so much more than whether or not you make it to your wedding night a virgin.

God's story of sex is so much bigger and so much more profound than the mere act of two people having sex. God uses sexuality at all stages of life to illustrate His love for His people, the church. It might seem strange, especially since any discussion of sex and sexuality is stereotypically seen as taboo among Christians, but God gave us the gift of sex (and the guardrails He put in place around a sexual relationship) to help illustrate what He is doing to bring His kingdom to Earth.

If that sounds too crazy to be true, just take a quick perusal of the Scriptures. The Bible is full of passages where God uses the idea of marriage and a romantic relationship to describe His relationship with His people. His Word is filled with verses that describe the church as the Bride of Christ, and Jesus as the Bridegroom (see 1 Corinthians 11:2). To name a few examples, in Matthew 25:1–13, Jesus tells a parable of a bridegroom who leaves and returns in the middle of the night, and how some of the women are found waiting for his return, but some aren't ready and waiting. The women who are not ready aren't welcomed into the wedding celebration. Isaiah 62:5 compares the Lord rejoicing over us to a bridegroom rejoicing over his bride. John the Baptist says that he is not the Messiah but is coming ahead of him. He continues to articulate this by saying, "The Bride belongs to the bridegroom. The friend who attends the Bridegroom waits and listens for him and is full of joy when he hears the Bridegroom's voice. That joy is mine, and it is now complete" (John 3:28–29).

But why, out of all of the things He could have used, does God use sex and the institution of marriage as a method to teach us about His plans for His children? The simple answer is, we are His image-bearers. Genesis 1:27 says, "So God created mankind in his own image, in the image of God he created them; male and female he created them." Our very core, our very identities on this earth as daughters and sons of the King of kings bear the image of God. And so, if purity is the pursuit of Christ on this earth, then what is a more perfect analogy for God's love and plans for His Church than to describe the salvation and eternity He plans to spend with His image-bearers by using the analogy of marriage and a bridegroom returning to take his beloved bride home? God uses our pursuit of Him as a way to continually purify and show His love for us—and that pursuit includes our sexuality.

But the even better news is, God's story of sex isn't just for people who are married—because God's children don't consist of only married people.

And God's story of sex isn't just for virgins, because God's kingdom is full of people who have had sex outside of marriage, have cheated on their significant other, have lost a spouse or have gone through a divorce, or have had their ability to make their own choices about their sexuality taken away because of violence, sexual assault, or rape. If God's story of sex—meaning the big analogy He uses to explain His love for His Church, His plans for redemption, and bringing forth the kingdom of heaven—was only for married people to experience, it would take out a lot of the power we all have as His image-bearers. It would lessen the importance of pursuing purity, and it would exclude a huge swath of believers from experiencing a part of this story Jesus came to Earth to tell. We are *all* image-bearers of Christ, and God uses each stage of our lives to help tell His story of sex and illustrate the amazing love He has for us.

Our God is a God of creation and a God of redemption. He uses the entire world and all of His creation to tell the story of His love and the plans He has for us. Sex and the pursuit of purity aren't any different. When we understand that purity is a person, we can remove the fear and shame from sex without falling prey to our culture's "anything goes" attitude. God tells amazing stories in our lives, and His story of sex is one that is too wonderful to miss out on. In this book, Josh and I hope to help you better understand God's intention and plan for sex, sexuality, and purity, but most importantly, how all of these aspects point directly back to Him and His plans for His kingdom.

# CHAPTER THREE

# FIXING YOUR GAZE

## JOSH

Imagine going on a road trip along the Blue Ridge Parkway, America's longest linear park that runs 469 miles through Virginia and North Carolina linking Shenandoah National Park to Great Smoky Mountains National Park. You are never in a rush (the speed limit is 45 MPH) and the views are breathtaking. It's not just a beautiful drive; there is a lot to do—from hiking trails, gem mines, and caverns, to restaurants, wineries, and so much more. If you ever get a chance to experience even a small portion of the Blue Ridge Parkway, you absolutely should. It's an amazing journey and unlike any other road trip.

However, the weather can change in an instant and, without much notice, you can go from a sunny, warm day to clouds, fog, rain, ice, and snow. It's not a wild assumption that your scenic road trip could go from 100 percent visibility to zero visibility within a day. Suddenly, your journey that looked so effortless at the start becomes a bit harder than you anticipated, and you start wondering if it's even worth the struggle. You might find yourself wondering if you can make it up or down the mountain, thinking if you just exited the parkway a bit before an official exit, you could avoid the inclement weather and find comfort and solace. But of course, most of us don't do that because we know that pulling to the side with limited visibility isn't the safest decision. In fact, I'm sure we've all been in a difficult situation, seen someone do something wildly illegal and dangerous to circumvent the elements, and yelled at the driver (or at least thought to yourself) something like, "What are you doing?! Are you *crazy*?!" It's because we know that the rules of the road, traffic laws, and basic guardrails on roads are there to keep us safe.

This is the same idea when it comes to God's plan and His intentions regarding sex in our lives. As stated earlier, purity is indeed a relationship, not an achievement, but that doesn't mean we simply get to do nothing and just receive the gift of purity. That's not how relationships work, after all. We don't have to do anything to receive God's love, and we are always His children, even when we mess up. However, as a follower of Christ, we are called to live differently. We are instructed to follow God's teaching when it comes to how we live. God has set out a path of purity we are to walk on. His teaching, His guidance, and the things He tells us to avoid are all meant to guide us and keep us on this path. And while we can't ever lose Christ's love and grace, we certainly will miss out on a lot of the good God has for us if we ignore the guardrails and instructions He gives us.

That's why we use the term "guardrails" a lot when we talk about the boundaries, rules, instructions, and teaching God gave us in the Bible. Just like the Blue Ridge Parkway, God set up some rules to keep us safe on our journey. God's way and the guardrails He places aren't there to be a bummer or a rule just for the sake of having a rule. They are there to keep us safe and keep us on the path of purity. That doesn't mean we won't encounter difficulties and challenges, but when we follow those rules, we're trusting that both the journey and the destination are worth any hardships.

The pursuit of purity is a process, and as God guides our steps, we have to decide if we truly trust His plan for our lives. While the natural instinct might be to immediately say, "Of course, I trust God's plan," stop and think about what that really means a bit more deeply. When you think about the instructions and the boundaries that God set up for us in the Bible, how do you perceive those? Do you look at God's instructions in a similar way as you might see guardrails on a highway, wishing it was okay to just zip off the road and get around traffic? Or do you really understand that His ways are ultimately better and safer for staying on course? Do you see it as a California native might look at a drive on the winding and steep Pacific Coast Highway—cool in theory, especially for outsiders, but ultimately too much trouble to be worth it? Or do you see it as a speed limit sign on a country road with no other cars around—a pointless rule only to slow you down and make the drive a bit more cumbersome?

That's where we really have to commit to trusting God's way, and where we have to truly confront what we believe about God and His story of sex, which is better than the world's. Jesus made purity possible for us, but in order to fully experience it in our own lives, we need to trust that God has our best interests in mind. Do we sincerely believe God is telling a better story? Do we completely trust that He's put up guardrails for a reason other than to stop us from having fun? Do we look at His instructions and follow His guidelines because we begrudgingly think, *Well, it is the right thing to do*, or do we believe it is better and more life-giving to follow the path He has for us? After all, if God is the Author of our lives, do we think

He's mapped out a boring textbook for us to follow, or do we think He has us on a thrilling adventure? Or, to say it more frankly, do we think God is the source of joy or a killjoy?

This is why Dan and I say that the pursuit of purity is a relationship, because our pursuit of purity—and more specifically, of Jesus—is compelled by a story. And not just *any* story, but an amazing, life-changing one. Think about any epic tale you've read where the main character sets out to leave their homeland to seek treasure, answers, or a new home. Why do they leave? Because a story has compelled them to go and search. That is what our pursuit of purity is—we are compelled by an amazing story to follow after Jesus. He is the Author of our faith, and He's the best Author out there.

## ENCOUNTERING JESUS

For those who place their faith in Jesus, purity is possible—but it's also a process. If we want to truly trust Him and truly understand and accept the better story He's writing, there must be an encounter with Him. How can we trust Him to purify us if we don't truly know Him, and how can we trust that the boundaries set up in our lives are for our own good if we don't encounter the One who put them up in the first place? We see all through the Bible where people are changed after an encounter with Jesus, and how that one interaction spurs them on to live differently and follow Him. And while each of those stories are powerful, let's focus on one in particular found in Mark's Gospel.

In chapter ten, we see a blind man named Bartimaeus sitting on the side of the road begging. When he learns Jesus of Nazareth is coming his way, Bartimaeus cries out to Jesus, saying, "Jesus, Son of David, have mercy on me!" (Mark 10:47). Chances are, if you've been going to church for any amount of time, you've heard the general story of Jesus healing a blind man. But let's break down why that encounter was so powerful and what it has to do with this journey we're embarking on together.

Bartimaeus knew who Jesus was—he really knew. While word had likely begun to spread about a man teaching and healing, Bartimaeus didn't just call Jesus a rabbi or a healer; he called Him the Son of David. That means he knew the Bible prophesied that the Messiah was to come from the line of David. Bartimaeus knew his Bible. He knew what line the Messiah was said to descend from, and he knew that person would be the restoration and redemption promised in Isaiah 62:1–2. In fact, Jesus Himself reads that Scripture in Luke 4 while attending synagogue, and when He finishes reading, He tells those in attendance that the Scripture is "fulfilled in your hearing" (Luke 4:21).

While the verses from Isaiah are powerful and paint the picture of a loving God and Savior coming to redeem and restore the broken, it also mentions something that was particularly important to someone like Bartimaeus. As we see in Luke 4:18, the section Jesus reads from Isaiah states not only that Jesus is the Messiah but that He is also the One who proclaims "recovery of sight for the blind."

So when Jesus crosses Bartimaeus's path, it makes sense that he doesn't waste any time calling out to Him. Here before him is the Messiah! The one that was prophesied to come and restore the world, heal the sick, and give sight to the blind. So naturally Bartimaeus cries out for Jesus, even when those around him tell him to be quiet (see Mark 10:48). But he doesn't stop calling after Jesus. Bartimaeus knows who He is, and this was an encounter too life changing to miss. And now after decades of hearing the story of the One who was coming to make everything right, here Jesus is, right in front of him. It was in that moment—in the midst of that encounter with Christ—that Bartimaeus was able to experience who Jesus is and "jump to his feet" and go to Him (v. 50).

This story would be amazing if it simply ended with Bartimaeus being healed. But so much more happened. Through Bartimaeus's response, we see the way Jesus and His grace tell a story so unlike anything we've ever heard, that it compels us to embark on a lifelong journey to know Him more through daily repentance and renewal. After Bartimaeus got Jesus' attention and He asked what He could do for him, Bartimaeus says in verse 51, "Rabbi, I want to see," and Jesus heals him. But that isn't all He does. In verse 52 we see Jesus respond, saying, "'Go . . . your faith has healed you.' Immediately he received his sight and followed Jesus along the road."

That encounter with Jesus didn't just restore Bartimaeus's sight, it changed his life. That encounter gave Bartimaeus a glimpse of Jesus and what He was trying to do here on Earth. It gave Bartimaeus a glimpse of the story Jesus was trying to tell all of us, and Bartimaeus couldn't help but get up and follow Him. It set him on a new life journey.

When Dan and I say purity is a relationship, the takeaway from this story is what we mean. While Jesus might not be physically crossing our paths the way He crossed Bartimaeus's, a lot of us might find ourselves in a similar situation. Like Bartimaeus, many of us have grown up hearing Christian teachings, or at least have spent the last few years learning about what it means to follow Jesus. Yet, in the middle of it all, the message of sex and purity has blurred the truth behind God's story and God's plan for our lives. As a result, we might think we need to do something to reclaim or keep our purity, we might spend years misunderstanding God's plan, and we might struggle to understand or fully trust God's story for us because of those misleading teachings.

But here is the wonderful news: if God is truly our hope, the perfector and finisher of our faith, and the One who purifies us, we only need to have an encounter with Him. Just like Bartimaeus only needed to call out in faith to Christ as He passed by, so do we only need to reach out to Jesus, trust and accept the salvation and relationship He offers, and follow Him. Because He isn't just the Author of our story—He is also the one that not only ensures the amazing completion of our story, but He Himself is the culmination and the end of our story. Our journey isn't about pursuing something; it's about pursuing Him.

God calls us to Himself, and He is faithful and good. We don't do anything to purify ourselves. It's all on God who will see to it that we are completely purified and that we will finish the journey—the pursuit—that He has set before us. Hopefully, this makes you breathe a sigh of relief. It's possible to stay on the path of purity because we aren't in charge of losing or keeping it in the first place. It's God working in us!

We need to step away from the lies, distortions, or half-truths we've been told about God's plan for sex. We need to do away with the beliefs that keep us from truly knowing the designer behind all things—including sex and the sexual union made for us—and encounter Jesus. Because when we do, we are drawn to the One who will see us through our faith journey and our pursuit of purity. Understanding Jesus and trusting the story He is telling are what will compel us to change course, pursue Jesus, and pursue purity through Him. When we strive for purity that doesn't come with that kind of relationship with Him, our journey gets muddled.

## A BETTER STORY

Jesus isn't here to purify only our bodies, which is why we make a clear distinction between purity and virginity. When Jesus calls us to purity, He also wants to purify our minds, our hearts, and our souls. It is because of this, purity doesn't hinge on our wedding night but rather on what Revelation 19:9 calls "the wedding supper of the Lamb," which is when we finally begin eternity with Christ. In essence, that means that while we're being purified in an eternal sense, Jesus works in us while we're still on the earth. Just as we pursue Jesus and strive to be more like Him every day, so too is He purifying us every day. It turns purity into a meaningful, deep relationship with the Creator of all things, and it turns purity from a race to the altar and the wedding night into a lifelong pursuit we *all* must embark upon, whether dating, married, single, divorced, or widowed.

Think about the "birds and bees" talk you heard as you grew up, probably mostly among your peers. Did you feel as though you were told about sex in a way that was meant to scare you or make you feel ashamed? Did discussions about sex confuse you or leave you feeling torn between what the culture around you said and what you were told in church?

We so often see polar opposite messages being thrown about everywhere. Our culture essentially says that anything is fair game as long as two consenting adults are a part of it. Meanwhile, the church locks down the conversation and offers what is likely not ill-intentioned but incomplete, painting sex to be something you shouldn't think about in any way until marriage. But if purity is about a relationship, and it is Jesus who does the purifying, what does that mean about how we handle sex and the sexual union in our own lives?

This leads me to talk now about a better story of sex and how God uses it and the sexual union to tell a bigger story. Sex isn't just a method to continue the human species, and it isn't something we spend our life waiting to experience on our wedding night. God intended sex to be a way for Him to communicate something to us, His people, throughout the span of our entire lives. Sex, sexual stewardship, and the sexual union are ways God tells us an important story every day of our lives.

We don't just need to reframe the way we talk about purity; we need to rediscover God's story of sex. We've been told that purity is synonymous with virginity, and once you've messed up, you're always damaged goods. We've been told that we must save ourselves to unlock a strange achievement on our wedding night after we've just spent our entire lives until that point ignoring and stifling our desires. But that was never God's intention. God's story of sex is one that spans our entire lives, our purity is solely found in the encounter and pursuit of Jesus, and God uses the different stages of our lives and sexual stewardship to teach us a key piece of His love for His people. To get a better idea of what He is trying to communicate to us, we have to jump into the Scriptures. So in Part Two, we are going to dig a bit deeper and break God's story of sex into four parts, or the Four Ps, as we call them: Proclamation, Protection, Pleasure, and Procreation. These four parts will help us understand the lifelong scope of God's story of sex and how we can live out this amazing story regardless of what stage we find ourselves in.

PART TWO:

# GOD'S STORY OF SEX

# CHAPTER 4

# PROCLAMATION

## DAN

Understanding that purity is a relationship, not an achievement, and that God is telling an amazing story through sex and the sexual union is a pretty drastic perspective shift for many of us. So let's look more closely at this story that God is telling and how He is using every one of us at every stage of our lives to tell a beautiful, life-changing story. Specifically, let's take a closer look at what we call the four Ps, the four pillars that help us outline God's story of sex: Proclamation, Protection, Pleasure, and Procreation.

Why do the four Ps paint a better and more accurate picture of God's plan for sex? Instead of being a set of rules to follow, they are a celebration of the beauty of this gift God has given us. The entire point of reframing our view of purity and God's intention behind sex isn't about teaching us what rules we can and cannot follow. It's helping us better understand God's plan, the role He wants us to play in that plan, and how we can be a part of the amazing work He is doing here on Earth. Once we understand His plan, those guardrails He puts up for us will start to make a lot more sense. And even better, as you can see, we're kicking things off with a proclamation.

It might seem strange to start with a proclamation rather than end on one, but that's part of the hope we've got in Jesus. We know that Jesus will be victorious in the end and that, despite all of the hardships we face in this life, as Christ followers, we'll get to spend eternity with Jesus. Ultimately, we know how this story is going to end—spending an eternity with Jesus. We can wake up every morning with renewed hope in the grace we receive from our relationship with Him, and we know that "neither height nor depth, nor anything else in all creation, will be able to separate us from the love of God that is in Christ Jesus our Lord" (Romans 8:39).

We're His! The battle is already won, so while we still might have a way to go before we are with Jesus forever in paradise, we know that we're going to make it there. Even if we don't fully understand what God's better story of sex is just yet, we know where God's story leads us to, and that's with Him, forever. That's why we're kicking things off with a proclamation! God is good, He gives good gifts, He's always in control, and forever full of love and grace for His children, regardless of their stage of life, the mistakes they've made, or how they've been hurt. And the same is true when it comes to the story He's telling us through sex and the sexual union.

Not only does this proclamation come with an immense amount of hope, it encompasses all of the other Ps combined. This is the pillar where we really get to the meat of the story God is telling us. To put it plainly, God uses sex to serve as a picture of Christ and the church. It's a story that He begins telling with the dawn of creation in Genesis when He formed us in His image (see Genesis 1:27), and it leads all the way to the "marriage supper of the lamb" (Revelation 19:7) when we get to spend eternity with Him in heaven.

That's quite a proclamation! Just as we've seen with purity, many of us in the church grew up hearing a lot of different perspectives of the purpose of sex. Sometimes it was presented as something we just shouldn't think about or worry about until we were officially married. Some of us heard that it was really only for having children. Others might have heard that it was necessary to keep humanity going but something almost shameful that shouldn't be talked about. For many it became a holy grail of sorts to obtain after years of abstinence, and for others it felt like a gift that God had only given to other people as they waited patiently to find a spouse. But much like we've sold purity short, we sold sex short too. God is doing something far greater here, because He isn't using sex to punish us, annoy us, or give us a fun way to keep the species going. God uses sex, the sexual union, and our pursuit of purity through Jesus at every stage of our lives to illustrate Christ with His Bride, the church.

It means that these guardrails that are put in place to guide how we engage in romantic relationships aren't meant to be too challenging to bear, they aren't meant to instill shame or fear, nor are they meant to generally be a bummer. They're there to keep us on track on this journey to see Christ's love for His Church played out in our very lives. And because we see a piece of that story played out in every phase of our lives, it offers a much-needed perspective shift to those of us who don't get married until later in life (if at all), those who have walked through divorce, those who have dealt with infidelity or sex outside of marriage, those married couples with kids and without kids, and everyone in between. We all get a seat at the table, and God is using our lives right where we are to highlight an important part of His story.

This is what we're proclaiming: the amazing hope we have in Christ, and the wonderful story He's telling in each of our lives. Everyone has a part in this story, no one is left behind, and our worth is tied to so much more than being single or married. At this point, depending on the stage of life you are in, you may be feeling excluded from this conversation, so let's take a closer look at how the various stages in our life help illustrate the story God is telling us about Christ's love for His Church.

## SINGLENESS: HOPE AS A VERB

In both secular and sacred spaces, we spend a lot of time talking about finding "the one" and spending the rest of our days on Earth growing old beside the love of our life. We see it in movies, books, television shows, and music; so whether we find ourselves in a faith community or a secular space, "singleness" can sometimes take on an air of discomfort or embarrassment when you find yourself surrounded by couples at an event. Single people often find themselves in awkward situations where they are made to feel like they have to make excuses for not having a spouse or significant other. I'm sure we've all heard (or made) excuses such as, "I'm focusing on my career right now," or "I need to learn to love myself before I start dating again."

It can feel even more frustrating and isolating when there doesn't seem to be a good space for single people within the Christian community. Churches often gear their small groups and community events around whether or not a person is single or married, and after you pass a certain age threshold, suddenly the community groups and socializing events seem to get fewer and fewer. Though it's often unintentional, it can make the message that the church sends to single people become a pretty bleak one: there isn't really a place or community for you here until you're married.

Thankfully, that is incredibly far from the message Christ is intending to send. He has a very clear intention for our lives while we're single, regardless of how long we find ourselves without a spouse. Unfortunately, the church has made it seem as though being single is only meant to be a phase where we're marking time as we wait for our potential spouse. It can feel quite hopeless when your brothers and sisters in Christ unintentionally send you the message that you aren't quite complete, and you aren't quite ready for the bigger plans God has for His children until you walk down the aisle. However, hopeless is the furthest thing from Christ's mind when He looks at a single person. In fact, when we're single (regardless of how long we're single) we find ourselves smack in the middle of God's plan that has us living out the word "hope" as a verb. Yes, you read that correctly! God never meant for you and me to sit sadly by our windows, weepily waiting for our future spouse to find us so our lives can begin. In God's better story of sex, we're living out the verb form of the word "hope" when we're single. It's a stage all about hoping and preparing.

Now, does that mean you have to sit home alone on a Friday night, giddy with some supernatural hope while you're single? Does that mean that feelings of loneliness, a desire to have a romantic partner, or a desire to start a family are sinful? Of course not! Obviously, not everyone has a desire to get married, but a lot of us do, and it's not surprising. Humans are meant to be in community, and we seek out others to walk through life together. The desire to have a romantic relationship, the desire to start a family, the desire to be in amorous love with another person are how most of us are wired, so it's normal and okay to have those moments where you feel sad if that isn't your current reality.

What's important is what you do after those feelings of sadness and loneliness. Because God has a purpose for you right now, and He's telling a story through your life, even in the midst of feeling lonely. In essence, when we're single, living out the verb "hope" means that we're in a season of faithful endurance. We are waiting for our future spouse to come into our lives, or if we don't want to get married, we're waiting to build that life we've always dreamed of. Because God's teaching instructs us to save sex for marriage, it means that the option of biological children may be out of the question and can turn the phase of "waiting" into a feeling that you've not fully unlocked the human experience.

However, God intended for singleness and that time of faithful endurance to be one where we're not sitting around, sad and lonely at home. It's not a phase where we haven't fully experienced all that God has for us, nor a time when we should feel incomplete. It's a season when God teaches us about the faithful endurance His Church, His Bride, experiences as we wait for His return.

Just as it can be for many of us while we're single, waiting for Christ to return can feel lonely and painful. We live on an unwell Earth, and sometimes it can seem as though brokenness, corruption, sin, and pain are around every corner. We can easily find ourselves looking at our surroundings and feeling overwhelmed by the hopeless desire to just sit down and wait for Jesus to take us home. But we know that we are called to so much more in this life, so we keep working, faithfully waiting for God to call us home or for the day that He returns. And that's what we're called to while we're single. Whether we never want to marry, whether we desperately want to find our soul mate, or if we're just seeing what God has next for us, our single days are meant to live out hope as a verb. That means hoping for the day we meet our future spouse, hoping for the day when we have the life we've always wanted for ourselves, but most of all, embodying that hope we have as we wait for Christ to return.

Just as we're called to more in this life than sitting and waiting, the same is true for our single life. Being single doesn't mean we are sitting around waiting for our lives to start. Our single days are meant for sanctification in following Jesus and His teachings and service as we spend our days doing important kingdom work. God is using the state of singleness and waiting for a spouse as a way to teach us about waiting for God, following after God, and doing the work that needs to be done here on Earth. We say that singleness embodies hope as a verb because in that state of actively hoping for Christ's return, we are also doing and acting to bring that same hope to others.

It's unfortunate that we as Christians have inadvertently spread the message that singleness is a state of being incomplete or that you haven't fully reached a level of human love and compassion if you don't have a spouse. Because being single is the time when we see the reality of this proclamation most acutely: this life is finite. Jesus is coming back, and we need to do the work to tell others about Him and be the "hands and feet" of Jesus here on Earth so we're ready for that day when we get to spend eternity with Him. A single person has a lot more freedom to move and act and get elbow-deep in kingdom work that a person who is married and maybe has a child or two simply can't do. So while this isn't a competition of who is holier, single people or married people, we must remember to value seasons of singleness in our own lives and support the single people in our communities, because God is telling His beautiful story of His love for His Church just as profoundly and as beautifully as a happily married couple. And the lessons we learn from our time being single are ones that are far too important to gloss over because we love a good romance. Singleness is a proclamation of the hope we all have for Christ's return!

## DATING: THE JOY OF GROWING CLOSER

Of course, even if we might never marry, chances are, you're going to date someone at least once. And if you do ever want to ultimately settle down with a partner, you've got to begin with dating. While individual rules of what dating looks like might differ (outside of the explicit guardrails God has given us), dating can be a time that is both exciting and taxing. It is in that season that a lot of intense work happens.

You've probably heard jokes about how long you should wait before you fully "reveal your crazy" to someone you're dating. Well, I love this story from Whitney, one of my colleagues at pureHOPE. When she was in college, a friend started dating a guy and Whitney jokingly asked her how long she was going to "hide her crazy" from her new boyfriend. Over the first few weeks, Whitney watched as her friend was trying to put her best face forward in the relationship. When her boyfriend came over, she would have random, hilarious outbursts behind his back as she tried to keep her quirky side hidden. Over time, however, he saw through the act and embraced her fully, quirks and all—they eventually ended up getting married!

And while it's a funny thing to joke about, it's a real struggle to allow yourself to be that vulnerable with someone, and it is one of the things that makes dating so tough. When you're dating someone, you've got to decide how much of your heart you reveal to that person. And much like my college roommate, once things start to get serious, it can be hard to figure out a good rate at which to let the less-than-perfect parts of you out for your partner to see.

But as uncomfortable as it is to let yourself be vulnerable with someone else, the amazing thing is when you share something and the person you're dating doesn't run away. It's a relief when you say the thing you've been so scared to admit, when you finally confide your deepest, darkest secrets with the person you're dating, and they stick around. That's when the thoughts of dating start to turn from *Wow, I really like this person. I hope I don't mess this up*, to, I'm going to spend the rest of my life with them.

The same can be true in building a relationship with Christ. Just like in a dating relationship with another person, just because we find ourselves being pulled toward God, it doesn't mean that we'll accept the gift He offers of eternal life with Him. You can date someone and get really serious but break up; so too can you learn about God and the salvation we find in Jesus and decide to choose another path.

When things finally click and a dating relationship turns from that awkward and slightly uncomfortable stage to a deep and intimate knowledge of another person—and eventually into a strong love—that's when things get exciting. It's when we look at the person we've been seeing at a distance and begin to dream of what's next together—marriage, adventures, travel, family, and building a long, happy life together. In the same way, God uses that same phase of growing closer to mirror the "dating" phase we experience as we're exploring our faith and deciding if we're ready to accept Christ's gift of salvation. It's where we look at what we see in the Bible, we listen to the accounts of other believers, we meditate on the things God has revealed to us, and we start thinking of what could come next. If we did decide to welcome Jesus into our hearts, what would that next stage of life look like? God uses dating to show us the part of His story where we begin to open ourselves up to Him and really start to think about a life lived for the glory of God.

## ENGAGEMENT: CHRIST'S BETROTHED

The engagement period can be a really fun and exciting time in a romantic relationship. You're engaged, you're planning your life together, you're planning your wedding and your honeymoon, and you're finally making real plans for your life together rather than just dreaming. You're closer than ever to the oneness you'll experience in marriage, but there is still a lot of work to be done to get ready for that moment. And despite the fact you've chosen to spend the rest of your life with your fiancé, you still find yourself learning new things about them every day.

As followers of Jesus, this is where we find ourselves right now. We've decided to give our lives to Christ and spend our time on Earth following His teaching, but until we are in heaven with Him, we're still separated from Him. And while we still have a lot of work to do here on Earth, and we spend every day learning more about Christ, the great news about this phase of our Christian life is that we're officially on track for an eternity in paradise with Jesus. The work He did on the cross has covered each of us, and by deciding to walk through life with Jesus as our Savior, we know that at the end of this life we're headed to an eternity with Him.

God uses the engagement phase of a relationship in His better story of sex to reveal His love for His people because it so perfectly encapsulates life on Earth as a Christian. There's an immense amount of joy and relief during an engagement as you get to bask in feelings of satisfaction that you've found the one person you've been looking for. However, there are still expectations at this stage of your relationship. There are obvious ones such as remaining faithful to your betrothed and continuing to be a good partner for him or her. However, there are other expectations that might be new for this particular phase. Now that the idea of spending the rest of your lives together is about to become a reality, it means you've got to start getting ready. You need a place to live and probably some furniture and home supplies, so you start a gift registry (or start stocking up on your own). You have to decide where you want to go for your honeymoon and when you want to take that trip. You need to start discussing finances together (if you haven't done this already) and start working on a budget. If you're going to change your last name, you need to figure out the steps needed for that; you need to learn about obtaining a marriage license; then there's planning and decorating the wedding and reception; and you've got to spread the word by making and sending invitations and save-the-date cards. Beyond that, if you're a Christ follower, there are the added expectations that you don't live together or have sex until after you're married.

It can feel like a lot of rules, and some of them might feel like a pointless exercise in waiting or bowing to the cultural expectations and mindsets of "We know we're going to be together forever. Let's just move in together now." "Do we really need to talk about money now? Can't we just do our own thing and sort of take things as they come when we're married?" "Why do we need to put new dishes and flatware on our registry when we already have some? Can't we put something more fun or practical on our list like a new television or cash?" "I'm obviously getting married to you, so I clearly love you and want to spend the rest of my life with you. Why do you care that I want one more night of meaningless fun?"

But here's why this stuff matters: it's all a part of building that lifelong relationship. And while some of the questions listed above are a bit trite, many of them speak to a really important concept that you have to accept when you're engaged and that you and I need to accept as we look at our time on Earth as followers of Jesus. That idea is that even though we might know the next phase of our story, we're not there yet, and we have to make the most of our time leading up to that awesome union to come.

While people do break off engagements, it's more common that once you're engaged, you're going to make it to the altar. You have a strong idea where you and your future spouse are headed, and it can feel really tough to wait to get to that next phase of your relationship. In fact, sometimes it can even feel like you're just wasting time. But it's just as valuable as the time you spent dating, and it's going to be just as life-giving as your future marriage. Protecting your relationship during your engagement, abiding by those guardrails and boundaries, and ensuring that you're doing the work to continue building the trust and love you have for your fiancé while also doing the practical work you need to get done before you officially marry are important. Whether you've got a long engagement or a short one, that period of time is where you are very excited about what's to come, but you know you still have work to do and lessons to learn.

It's the same in our walk with Christ. We know we're heaven bound, but this time on Earth isn't meaningless. We've all likely heard a well-meaning but misled Christian in our lives shrug off or minimize the work we're called to do here on Earth in the face of heaven. And while, yes, our main goal is eternity with Christ, we have to remember that we're here right now for a reason. This moment is one where we continue to learn and grow in our relationship with God. It's that daily purification we've spent so much time talking about. But practically, there's stuff we've got to get done here as well. We're called to spread God's message to all corners and all people of this earth. We're called to feed the hungry, clothe the naked, and care for the widow and the orphan. Sure, all things will be made whole in heaven, but Jesus commanded us to do that work of spreading His message and to be a conduit for the restoration that only He can bring to the people on Earth here and now.

As Jesus followers, we're promised an eternity with Him. It's a done deal. The price has been paid, and we're officially betrothed to our Bridegroom. However, if we blow off this time on Earth, if we waste it by not doing the work to draw closer to God and to do our best to follow where He leads us in this life, we might not be losing our salvation, but we're losing a beautiful and vital part of our relationship with Him. And we see the importance and the beauty of this proclamation through the season of being engaged, however long that period might last.

## MARRIAGE: HOPE AS A NOUN

When we're single, God uses that time to show us what it's like to live in a stage of waiting, seeking, and excitement of what's to come: hope as a verb. But marriage is meant to show us what it's like to experience hope as a noun. Marriage is the fulfillment of our journey trying to find a spouse—we've found "our person," and we've made our promise to one another official, before God and our communities. It's when we can finally experience that unfettered oneness and closeness with the person we've grown to love through dating and being engaged. Becoming an official husband and wife is something that we celebrate with those we love the most, because it's a big deal. We take our vows in front of family and friends where we promise to remain faithful and to love and care for each other. Then we all hang out and celebrate this new union together. It's something that is very special because a marriage is a signifier that where there were once two people, there is now one. Scripture says it this way: "That is why a man leaves his father and mother and is united to his wife, and they become one flesh" (Genesis 2:24). No one was erased, but now these two individuals have linked arms and have committed to travel through this life together, working for one common goal rather than two individual ones. Not only do a husband and wife find their lives intertwined with things like combined finances, living together, and actively building a future together, but they are able to experience that physical closeness and oneness that come from the sexual union.

This oneness is representative of the culmination of the story God is telling us. Marriage is a representation of that hope we were living out as we waited for Christ. Marriage represents the intimate closeness we'll have with our Father in heaven once this world has passed away. It's something we have to wait for, yes, and waiting is hard, but once we get there, we'll find that the waiting was very much worth it.

It can be easy to look at our lives and wonder why God cares about when we start having sex, why He cares about living together before marriage, and why He cares about things such as the journey our romantic relationships take us. It's because of this! Because marriage, dating, and sex aren't just arbitrary acts that we experience based on cultural expectations. God uses the phases of our life—singleness, dating, engagement, and marriage—to show us how He loves us and the plans He has for us. That is why we have the guardrails we do—because the journey He has us embarking on is meant to mirror the journey we'll embark on as we move closer to Jesus and ultimately spend the rest of our lives with Him in heaven.

This is why purity is far more than a race to get to your wedding night as a virgin, and it's why sex matters to us at all. Because, as odd as it might sound at first, sex is a form of worship. Our bodies are the temple of the Holy Spirit, and that doesn't stop being true at any point in our lives. So just as the ancient temple in Jerusalem was continuously made pure to be a holy and acceptable place for God to dwell, you and I must allow Jesus to daily purify us. By paying attention to the boundaries He's placed for us and following His teachings, we will stay on track to live out exactly what He has planned for us.

This isn't meant to be a message that frustrates single people. Because while the metaphor God is playing out in our lives culminates in a wedding, it's important to remember that He not only has a purpose and a plan for those of us who are single, but also His decision to welcome us into His kingdom doesn't hinge on our marital status. Living out the single life in faithfulness, obeying God's teachings, and working to do as He commands here on Earth are vital work we can't shrug off. While you might be in the stage of singleness here on Earth, in the story God is telling, as a Christ follower, you're living in that engagement period—we all are. That means your life is important, it has meaning, and you've got holy work to do. While God does indeed use the journey toward marriage and the sexual union as a metaphor to tell the story of His love for His Church, you can experience that story firsthand—it doesn't mean you're not included in that story if you yourself aren't married. You're a child of God. You've been saved by grace, and you are heaven bound. Jesus is your Bridegroom, and whether you're single and love it or you're single and hate it, don't let anyone (especially yourself) tell you that your life is somehow sad, incomplete, or less important than those in serious relationships or marriages around you.

That's why Josh and I are kicking off the Four Ps with a proclamation of this amazing story God is telling. It means that the phases of life, the guardrails, and the teachings all have a purpose and a part to play in a larger story. However, because our lives are a part of God's larger story, it also means that we're called to be faithful and to do our best to seek after Christ to bring His love to the world. Single, married, divorced, dating, engaged—it doesn't matter. As Christ followers, we're all called to prioritize His teachings for our life and bring His truth to others. We can see the amazing story God is telling through romance and marriage and the sexual union, but experiencing that firsthand does not give married believers an extra dose of holy understanding, nor does it mean single Christians should have less of a seat at the table. As Christ followers, we're all in the middle of that "engagement" stage in our walk with the Lord, and we're all working to be a good steward of the time and talents He has given us until we're one day called home for that big wedding celebration with our Bridegroom. What an amazing proclamation that is!

# CHAPTER 5

# GUARDRAILS ARE GOOD

## JOSH

Now that we've explored the proclamation of what God's better story of sex is meant to teach us in the different stages of our life, let's begin exploring more ways God uses marriage and the sexual union to tell a better story. It's time to explore the second of the Four Ps: Protection.

When we think of the purpose of sex, the first word that comes to mind probably isn't "protection." So why is it the second pillar we bring up when explaining God's better story of sex? To answer that question, we first have to understand another word—"*covenant*." "Covenant" is a word that we hear a lot, sometimes in conjunction with biblical stuff, sometimes in conjunction with marriage, and sometimes it pops up in random places like your Homeowners Association Agreement. But the way we're going to be using the word is in describing a profound promise with expansive importance that is made between individuals and God. Some covenants you might be most familiar with from the Bible are ones such as God's covenant with Noah never to flood the entire earth again, God's covenant with Abraham that He would make him into a "great nation" (Genesis

12:2), and God's covenant with the Israelites after freeing them from Egypt. Of course, we also cannot forget the covenant we have with Jesus after He died on the cross for our sins, allowing us to have a personal relationship with God and providing us an eternity with Christ.

To God, everything starts with covenant. It's an agreement, a promise, and a sense of security that we have in Him. God keeps His promises; it's proven all throughout the Bible. So when He says our debts have been paid and we can rest in the salvation we have in Christ, we know it's true. Those covenants allow us to feel safe while in God's control, and it helps us trust that He has our best interests at heart. So when we move through our lives and we encounter trouble, we can lean on the promises He made to help us get through the hard times.

It isn't surprising, then, to see that God has used that same structure when it comes to marriage and sex. The importance of covenant is why God has placed so much importance in saving sex for marriage. It can feel strange to save sexual intercourse for marriage when you find yourself engaged. After all, you're going to get married, you're going to make that commitment—what difference is there if you and your fiancé have sex during your engagement or if you wait only a few more months until your wedding night? The difference is the covenant you make on your wedding day.

As we discussed in the last chapter, marriage, sex, and the sexual union are intended to be a metaphor, a proclamation of the story that God is telling of His love for His Church. The fear of death and what happens when we die is a pretty common metaphor, but as followers of Christ, we don't have to be afraid. We can rest in the assurance that we are God's children, and because of that we'll spend eternity in heaven with Him. So the same way we find security and safety in the covenant we have with

God—thanks to Jesus' sacrifice on the cross—He wants us to feel that same security with our spouse in the covenant of marriage before we experience physical intimacy.

Ultimately, sex is incredibly intimate, so it's an act that makes two people exceptionally vulnerable within their relationship. God designed it as something that can help foster unity, safety, and security, and the best way to achieve that is under the protection of the marriage covenant. Being physically intimate with a spouse isn't just a way to have a fun time; it's also a way to increase that connection and love you have for each other. And when physical intimacy happens in the context of marriage, it becomes a reminder of the covenant each of you made on your wedding day. It becomes a physical expression of saying, "I still do," days, months, and years after your wedding day when you first said your vows.

## FOSTERING SAFETY

Feeling truly safe in a relationship—safe enough to be this intimate with a person—goes beyond feeling secure in the status of the relationship. If physical intimacy is meant to be analogous to our oneness with God, then it should be treated with that level of respect and sacredness. That means not only saving sex for marriage but treating it as something meant to build up your partner and increase your connection to each other. Sex should never be used as a way to tear down, cause hurt, or make your spouse feel unsafe.

This means that sex within the confines of marriage, just like our oneness with God in heaven, is based on communication and mutual respect and understanding. So first and foremost, sex isn't something that should be used as a way to hurt or manipulate your spouse, nor should it be something used to assert dominance. In short, sexual assault, rape, and molestation—even when these acts are found within a marital relationship—are total perversions of God's better story of sex. If your partner says no to intercourse and you force yourself on them, try to "wear them down," or manipulate them into feeling badly for not being in the mood, you're not creating an environment of safety. That isn't how God intended a marriage relationship to be.

We're also not creating a safe environment when sex is something used to coerce or manipulate our partner to get our way. It's a trope you see frequently in television and movies, where one spouse wants something or wants the other to admit to wrongdoing and will stop all sexual intercourse until their partner acquiesces. While this doesn't cause physical harm, it manipulates your spouse into doing things your way, which in turn damages the intimacy and vulnerability you started to cultivate on your wedding day.

In 1 Corinthians 7:5, the Bible says, "Do not deprive each other except perhaps by mutual consent and for a time, so that you may devote yourselves to prayer. Then come together again so that Satan will not tempt you because of your lack of self-control." The important word in this verse is "consent." It's the key that hinges on maintaining the protection we feel. What consent means is that both of you have a voice, and both of your feelings and opinions matter. When it comes to ultimate intimacy and oneness experienced in the sexual union, it's vital for both parties to feel as though their voice and feelings are being heard, respected, and cared for. When a husband and wife can come together feeling safe within their oneness, it doesn't just help them grow as a couple; it helps them fight off attempts the enemy will make to infiltrate their lives and their marriage with temptation.

By protecting our relationship, it means we're not only making sure to listen to our spouse when they say they aren't in the mood; it also means that we don't use sex as a bargaining tool or as a method to "teach him or her a lesson." When you deprive your partner in that way, you aren't protecting the relationship. Instead, you are manipulating your spouse and missing God's better story of sex. By doing that, you're fostering mistrust, which when allowed to fester in a relationship can often lead to its downfall.

However, just like you shouldn't deprive your spouse as a way to manipulate, it also means that the respect and consent must go in the other direction. Both in secular and sacred spaces, we often hear the message that a spouse (especially a wife) should never deprive his or her partner of sex. Even worse, we see messages spread that men are so driven by their sexuality that for a woman to say no to her husband's sexual desires even once, the husband will become disinterested, resentful, and won't feel respected.

A wife isn't under any obligation to immediately have sex again as soon as her physician gives the green light after childbirth. Sometimes a wife (or a husband) might feel exhausted after a long day of work, caring for the kids, or doing yard work, and they just want to go to bed. Or maybe one of you has a lot on your mind, and you just aren't feeling like you're in the right headspace. You shouldn't have to ignore those feelings; you don't have to "fake it till you make it" to keep a white-knuckle grip on your marriage. These are all perfect examples of when consenting to wait until another time is so important.

The way we protect our spouse and our marriage is by keeping communication lines wide open and creating a space where both parties feel comfortable saying exactly what's going on inside. To say that a wife must always give her husband sex whenever he asks is unfair to the wife, but it's also unfair to the husband. Painting our spouse out to be a sex-fueled monster who will leave the first time he's told no, or a grumpy prude who never wants to do anything fun, isn't protecting the relationship or one another, and it's not how God's story of sex was meant to play out.

Ultimately, if a husband and a wife are consistently open and honest with each other, and if neither uses the deprivation of sex as a manipulation tool, it changes the dynamic of intimacy. If sex is used as a way to increase intimacy, experience oneness with each other, and continue growing that love and trust, then when a husband or a wife suggests sex and the other says no, it's no longer something to be afraid of. When you both keep that communication, respect, and protection of the relationship and your spouse in the forefront of your mind, it's easier to really hear and read your spouse when they express a desire or when they aren't necessarily in the mood.

Sex is meant to be a picture of God's love and protection for His Church, so that means it should always stem from mutual respect and love and foster a feeling of safety at all times. It's vital that we implement that in the sexual union found in marriage, but it also means that we as a church should have a strong reaction to people who use sex to power grab, abuse, and cause pain. Rape, sexual assault, harassment, and sexual violence are a problem in every corner of the world as a symptom of this unwell Earth. However, the fact that this unwellness is something so prevalent in Christian communities (and worse, has frequently been covered up, ignored, or victims have been blamed to protect people in power) it should feel like a punch in the gut to all of us. Nothing on this earth is perfect, but shouldn't the church be one space where anyone can feel safe from sexual abuse?

Freedom from sexual brokenness, as well as living in and understanding God's better story of sex, starts with each of us. And one of those areas is fostering the protection we each should have over the sexual union. The

Christian community should be one of the most vocal communities against sexual violence, and a true harbor of safety for victims of sexual violence because at its core, our God created the sexual union as a way not only to show His love for His people but also to help us experience on Earth the safety and protection we have in Him.

## COVERING IN COMMUNITY

When sex is used outside of God's plan, when it is used to manipulate, exert power, hurt, or cause harm in general, it dismantles everything that God is teaching us through His story of sex. It's also isolating. Whether you find yourself in a marriage where sex is used as a bargaining tool or you've been the victim of abuse, those experiences can cause feelings of shame and of being alone. And as humans, we're not meant to be alone.

We've already touched on the fact that all humankind was created as male and female image-bearers of Christ (see Genesis 1:27). And as image-bearers, we have a responsibility here on Earth. Our actions are important, and as Christ followers, those actions point back to God. So it is important for us to protect our brothers and sisters in Christ and cover one another. It's why we say our marriage vows in front of our loved ones—to welcome in the support and covering from our brothers and sisters in Christ. God has called us to live in community with one another, and even more exciting, community is another form of protection that covers both married and single people.

Living as image-bearers and actively contributing and being a part of a group of believers isn't just about attending a church on Sundays. It's about investing in one another's lives. It's about dinners together. It's about trips together. It's about late nights talking about silly things and things that break your heart. It's about checking in on people you haven't heard from in a while. It's about asking questions when things seem off, holding one another accountable when we miss the mark, and standing beside each other in times of trial.

I think 1 Peter 4:8–10 says it best: "Above all, love each other deeply, because love covers over a multitude of sins. Offer hospitality to one another without grumbling. Each of you should use whatever gifts you have received to serve others, as faithful stewards of God's grace in its various forms."

Recently, I heard two very different stories about people's experiences within community. The first story was from a single young woman who was trying to plug in at her new church. I'll call her Rebecca. She found a Bible study for women who were around her age, and she had been attending faithfully every week. As the group grew closer, Rebecca still felt a bit like an outsider as the only single woman (who also had no kids), but she found the study interesting, so she tried to continue to bond with the other women. After a few months together, they decided they wanted to plan a fun group outing. Rebecca was really excited and suggested a few local outdoor attractions they could attend that could be accommodating in case the women with kids wanted to bring the children along. Suddenly, the room got quiet.

"We figured you'd watch the kids since you aren't married and don't have any children and probably don't need a day out," one of the women said awkwardly.

Rebecca didn't stay in that Bible study much longer.

The second story was from a young married couple; I'll call them Ken and Briana. They were looking to plug in at their local church several months before their wedding day. Their church had a small group meet-up event where people at different similar life stages sat at a table together for six weeks and, with the guidance of a program put on by the church, began to form a small group. Ken and Briana were still technically engaged, but there wasn't a table for engaged people. So they wandered over to the "young married" part of the room. When they sat at the table, they admitted their marital status to the other couples sitting there.

"You're close enough," one of the women at the table said. "It's just approximate life stages anyway. Stick around! We'd love to get to know you two!"

Ken and Briana felt instantly welcomed and sat down. The group ended up clicking incredibly well, and not only did Ken and Briana invite their newfound small group to their wedding a few months down the road, but ten years later, the group still remained close friends. That group walked through amazing events, like buying first homes, the birth of children, new jobs, and incredibly tough things, like the death of a parent after a long fight with Alzheimer's, miscarriages, lost jobs, and other big health scares.

In Rebecca's case, when she was thought not to be an important enough member of the community, she wasn't just hurt personally. It ultimately drove her away from the group and left her with some pain she had to work out with herself and the Lord down the line. It caused her not to trust married women as easily, and to automatically assume that as a single woman with no kids, she wouldn't ever find the close community she craved with other Christian women her age.

However, with Ken and Briana, even though they didn't totally meet the exact requirements for the group, they were welcomed. And starting things off with an air of welcome and acceptance—and creating a seat at the table for them where there wasn't a clear seat—helped them feel safe. It allowed the relationship to start off on a great foot, and Ken and Briana's guards were instantly taken down. It was the start of lifelong friendship and community. That community would go on to offer Ken and Briana support, love, and a group of people whom they could hang out with on the weekends or confide in during a season of trouble or heartbreak. That community also served as a protection, because Ken and Briana knew that these friends wouldn't be afraid to step up if they needed the help, but they also wouldn't keep quiet if they saw Ken and Briana heading down a dangerous path.

That's why we say that God's story of sex is so much more than a man and a woman getting married and staying virgins until marriage. It's why we say this story plays out in every stage of our life, and why we call purity a relationship rather than an accomplishment. Because when we boil down purity to something we think we can do for God, when we turn marriage into the ultimate goal, or when we turn sex into a tool that can be used to get our way in a marriage, we're not only distorting God's story of sex; we're leaving people behind. It's why protection is one of the key pillars to this story. If God wants us to see His love and plans for His children, He wants to make sure we're protected. All of us.

We are meant to look out for and protect our spouse, but we are also called to do that in our community of believers. And when we can honor and recognize the protection Christ set out for us within the covenants of marriage and salvation, it helps us see the beauty and the sacredness in them as well. It's another instance of how we can see the rules God laid out for us to follow when it comes to sex and the sexual union as guardrails. It's not just about sex or abstinence. It's about so much more, and it's about so much more than just one specific type of relationship. God is not only telling a broad and beautiful story; He is also helping us honor and protect the covenants we have made with our spouse, with our community, and with Him. When we see those guardrails and the protection, we can really relish in the freedom we have in Christ and the safety we have knowing our Father in heaven is always watching out for us. That same freedom and safety are things we can then transfer to the covenant we find ourselves under in our marriages and with our communities.

When we can see the proclamation of God's story of sex and the protection and ways it calls us to protect those in our community, we can start to see the amazing picture Christ is creating and calling us to be part of. It gives us a glimpse into the bigger story God is telling and the ways that it can be told through each of our lives, wherever we find ourselves. And the inclusive, welcoming nature of God's story should be a freeing one!

But now that we've set up the foundation for the bigger story God is telling, let's start diving into the last two of the Four Ps that focus more specifically on the marital relationship. As with everything in God's story, there are applications to each of us at all life stages, but the final two Ps, Pleasure and Procreation, are the two things most commonly associated with marriage and the sexual union.

# CHAPTER 6

# BECOMING ONE

## DAN

Here is the wonderful truth about sex: God created sex and the sexual union to tell a beautiful story that is much larger than a husband and wife, and He made the sexual union something that is meant to be pleasurable.

Unfortunately, our culture has fixated quite a bit on that piece of the puzzle. We live in a culture that calls for us not to hold ourselves back and do anything that feels good. You may have heard someone shrug off the story of someone's sexual encounter that fell outside the guardrails God placed for us by saying, "They're consenting adults. If it feels good, do it, right?" And while there is a lot we could unpack from a statement like that, it's important to look carefully at what is really being said.

Phrases such as "they're consenting adults" and "if it feels good, do it" are two great examples of how the enemy can expertly twist and distort God's story. Phrases like that often come in direct opposition to the narrative of fear and shame so many of us received about sex from churches. We have taken the beauty out of God's story of sex and boiled it down to a frenzied pursuit to "save yourself" for marriage and protect your own purity.

And because we changed sex into something that we should be afraid and ashamed of, the enemy jumped all over it with his own distortions, so naturally our culture has swung in the complete opposite direction. In an attempt to empower one another and validate the importance of sex and the sexual union without God's teachings and guardrails, we've moved to a perspective of "anything goes as long as it's between fully consenting adults."

So what is the real story here? Where is God's truth when it comes to the pleasure found in the sexual union? Let's think back to guardrails on a road for a moment. If you find yourself driving on a beautiful mountain pass in the wilderness, sometimes the road can seriously wind this way and that. Sometimes you can look at the terrain beyond the guardrails and think, *I'm not on a cliffside or anything. It's just wilderness over there. What would happen if I just hopped off the road and did some off-roading and drove straight through?*

Most of us probably don't get much further than that fleeting thought. Why haven't many of us seriously considered off-roading in the wilderness? Because as much as we might be tempted to take a more direct path to our destination, and as much as we might want to take a break from winding roads, we know those guardrails are there to protect us! And once we grasp that fact, the drive is a lot more fun knowing that the alternative is driving along the rocky terrain in a tiny sedan. Part of the joy of the journey is unlocked by the simple act of observing and respecting the guardrails.

It's the same idea with sex. Just as the covenant relationship of marriage is meant to provide a feeling of safety and protection, so too it is meant to evoke delight. God's covenant with humankind is meant to evoke delight in us, and it brings us all joy and fulfillment. So it's only natural that, as He tells that story of His love for His Church and His people, He highlights that delight with an earthly covenant—the one made between a man and a woman on their wedding day.

Does this mean that when a person has sex outside of the marriage covenant it isn't a pleasurable experience? Of course not. It's the whole reason there is even a discussion about God's plan for engaging in the sexual union: because it brings physical pleasure. However, a key aspect of what God intends for us to experience with sex is far more than just physical pleasure. He created sex to show us the fullness of delight, joy, safety, and pleasure that we can experience with someone in a covenant relationship. The unique intimacy and oneness that a husband and wife experience when they engage in the sexual union as opposed to a casual partner are why God created the guardrail of marriage.

As we've touched on a lot in this book, sex isn't just about the physical act between two people. Sex is a story—a massive, beautiful story of God's love for His people—so those guardrails are not only meant to keep us safe but also to keep us following the story He is trying to tell.

This doesn't mean we need to be embarrassed about the pleasure derived from sex. God designed it to be fun and to feel good! Again, it's meant to point to the joy and delight we will feel when we have that unfettered oneness with God in heaven. He designed for us to find security and an extra amount of intimacy, closeness, and pleasure when we engage in the sexual union within the boundaries of marriage, and He designed our bodies to enjoy the act. We are made to find pleasure in being touched, we are made to wonder and be amazed in that beautiful intimacy and deep connection we have with our spouse and express that in a physical way, and we are made to delight in the feelings that bring us all the way through that climax of physical connection.

Sex may be more than pleasure, but that doesn't mean pleasure isn't an important part of it. What is truly amazing about God's better story of sex is how He designed our bodies, our hearts, and our brains to engage with and feel the sexual union. Sex, as God intended it, is so much more than a fleeting good feeling. If that's all it was, the sexual union would be a pretty lousy metaphor for the ultimate delight and closeness we'll one day feel in heaven with Christ. Thankfully, it's so much more than that. When a husband and wife are physically intimate, it's not just a moment when they are physically close, and it isn't just about delighting in the physical sensations. When a husband and wife can come together and create a safe environment full of love and understanding, where the lines of communication are open, and each partner is not only concerned with their own pleasure but making their spouse feel safe and loved in the moment as well, an incredible bonding moment happens. God designed our bodies to respond with a huge dopamine rush during an orgasm, and our neuroplastic brains take that intense rush of physical pleasure and the influx of dopamine (or the "happiness hormone") and our bodies begin to create a bond with the person causing those feelings. That bond is meant to drive those two individuals to continually reinforce their attraction and desire for each other.

It's no wonder why bringing sex into a dating relationship can muddy the waters so quickly. When sex happens outside the covenant of marriage, we feel that rush of dopamine and that instinctual draw and desire for closeness with the person we're dating. However, the safety, security, and stability that are found within the protection of marriage aren't there.

This very real act of bonding due to the dopamine rush we receive during sex was an idea that I didn't hear until I was an adult sitting with a group of other men at church. Suddenly I could very clearly understand why so many of us who had sex with our partners felt so profoundly broken when the relationships fell apart, and why we had a tendency to drift back to our exes: because the sexual nature of our relationship had created an invisible bond between us, and breaking it off was incredibly hard and heartbreaking!

Sex outside of marriage makes the relationship cloudy and confusing and can make it even more painful should the relationship fall apart. The very pleasure we feel in sex is meant to continuously drive us closer and bond us more profoundly with our spouse. It's to give us a peek into the constant joy and closeness we will feel with God one day. If that bond is being sent out toward several different partners, it not only trains our brain to react to that physical need for bonding differently, but it also trains our hearts to discredit the need for closeness and intimacy with another person we are hardwired to feel during and after sex. It brings us a lot of pain that God never intended for us. Just as we will spend eternity growing ever closer with our one heavenly Father and triune God, the pleasure felt from that profound bond and closeness through sex is intended to be experienced with only our spouse. The great news is, God is a perfect Father, and just because we've experienced that bond with someone other than our spouse doesn't mean we're broken or eternally damaged goods. God can still restore us and heal that brokenness in our heart, and we can still go on to have just as meaningful and powerful of a bond with our spouse. However, understanding God's design for sex and His design for how our bodies react to sex can help us better understand why sex is best when experienced within a marriage covenant, and ultimately help us to be a better steward of our sexuality.

It's important to remember that God made this world, and He designed the earth with its color and beauty. We don't feel ashamed about reveling in the beauty of a gorgeous sunset or a beautiful view after a long hike, so we don't need to feel ashamed about enjoying the wonderful gift God gave us in the sexual union. Finding joy in that gift, finding joy in the guardrails and boundaries He has placed in our lives and the instructions He left us regarding how we should enjoy that gift, and the amazing story He's telling through it are just as meaningful and powerful as finding joy in other areas of beauty in God's creation.

## WHEN SEX CAUSES PAIN

We've touched on the fact that sex isn't ever meant to make someone feel unsafe or put someone in danger, but it needs to be said that sex isn't meant to bring another person pain. Pleasure is one of the pivotal points of God's story for sex, which means pain in sex contradicts God's plan. Just like using sex to assert power or instill fear in someone else is a perversion of God's story, it's also perverting His story when we use sex to cause pain.

As mentioned in the chapter about protection, communication is vital between a husband and wife. Listen to your spouse when they tell you how they're feeling about those intimate moments, and give your spouse grace and understanding if something is bringing them emotional or physical pain. For those who have experienced sexual violence, sometimes being touched a certain way or hearing certain words can trigger a traumatic memory and completely remove them from the loving, safe moment they are in with their spouse. Instead, it returns them to a memory of fear, trauma, and pain. Create a space in your relationship that allows that honesty and openness so if something like that comes up, you can address it and make your spouse feel safe again as soon as possible.

Likewise, there are some things that can cause your partner physical pain, regardless of your intentions to inflict pain. We live in a fallen world, so those things God intended to be fully pleasurable and beautiful are often marred by the natural brokenness of life. If one or both partners experience physical pain during sex, it doesn't mean you've fallen out of favor with God; it doesn't necessarily mean you're even doing anything wrong during the sex act. A lot of women report experiencing pain during their first time having sex. There are a litany of reasons why sex could potentially cause pain, and it's not something to be ashamed of. Conditions like vaginismus can cause sex to be incredibly painful for a woman, and Peyronie's disease can make sex painful for a man, but there are plenty of other things that can make sex painful for one or both parties, such as allergies, arthritis, sensitive skin, endometriosis, and a wide range of other medical conditions.

So what does all of this mean? Why, if God's better story of sex is built on a pillar of the experience of pleasure, are we talking so much about pain? The first reason is to dispel some of those harmful myths many of us heard from purity culture teachings. So many of us were promised that if we saved sex for marriage, sex in our married life would be amazing from day one. Unfortunately, that's not always the case. Mental and emotional blocks can make it hard to get into that vulnerable, intimate space needed to really enjoy the sexual union with your new spouse, not to mention the wide range of reasons sex might be a physically painful experience. It's a symptom of this fallen world, but that doesn't mean that if you or your spouse struggle with these things, you don't get to experience the pleasure that can come from the sexual union and the covenantal delight we experience in marriage. When a husband and wife enter into that covenantal relationship with one another and when they begin experiencing the sexual union, their goal isn't just to achieve their own pleasure—their goal becomes experiencing a deeper "oneness" in their marriage.

Part of what makes sex so meaningful is that oneness and closeness you feel with your spouse—it's why God uses it as a poignant metaphor for the oneness and closeness we'll experience with Him in heaven. As said earlier, sex shouldn't be used to manipulate, assert power, teach lessons, and generally cause harm, so it's up to us to keep those lines of communication open and make sure the grace and love we feel for our spouse are readily available. So if a husband or wife expresses any discomfort or pain during sex, it's vital that the two come together, discuss what is happening, and work to fix it together. Sometimes slowing down and communicating more effectively can fix the problem, and sometimes that pain will need to be worked through with a physician or therapist. The level of intimacy found within marriage is meant to point us to Christ, so caring for your spouse and listening to them when they express an issue is how you can treat the sexual union as the sacred thing it truly is.

## SINGLENESS AND PLEASURE

Of course, if you're reading this and you're single, you might be feeling a bit frustrated. Once again, here is something in the church designed to leave single people out, right? Wrong! We've said it again and again that God's story of sex is being told in every stage and every aspect of our lives. So God in no way has reserved pleasure for married folks only. There are many forms of pleasure God provides for His people; sex is only one of them.

Yes, the sexual union is intended only for marriage, so the physical pleasure derived from that act is reserved for married people. But we still get to experience that very real joy that comes from the covenant relationship with God and the closeness and safety we feel in Him. He designed the pleasure found from sex to point to His story and His love for us, but He's also created a lot of other areas in life that can bring us pleasure.

Understandably, that is probably a frustrating sentiment to read if you're single and you really don't want to be. However, it's important to remember that God has a plan and a purpose for each and every one of us, and that purpose goes way beyond whom we marry. He has given us a big, beautiful world to explore and a set of skills and talents that we get to use in this world for His glory. It can feel painful to be single when you always thought you'd be married at a certain point in your life, or if you're finding yourself single after a bad breakup, a painful divorce, or even death. But it's important to remember that God's plan and purpose for you didn't and never will hinge on your spouse. The way God delights in you has nothing to do with your spouse. And the good gifts that God gives to His children aren't only reserved for married people. God puts lots of instances of joy and pleasure in each of our lives, such as the seemingly innocuous moments of enjoying the beauty of His creation around you; the joy and safety you find in authentic community; the joy you find when you are able to do work or art that you find fulfilling; and the joy you find in your relationship with Christ, which can be adventurous.

So always remember that, while sex is intended to be experienced within the marriage covenant, it doesn't mean single people are called to live a life devoid of pleasure. God loves His children, and He's not going to put you on the shelf until someone puts a ring on your finger. It just means that the pleasure you get to experience on this earth will come from different outlets than the marriage covenant, and they are just as powerful, just as meaningful, and just as profoundly pointing to God.

God uses our lives at all stages to tell a story of how He constantly purifies us and how, as Jesus followers, we are promised an eternity with

Him. That is something that is so amazing and so beautiful! Regardless of what piece of the story you see played out in your life, one thing is certain: stepping into that truth, understanding and following the path Christ set before you, and seeing the story of God's love played out in your own life and the lives of those around you are profound. So with that in mind, let's end this section with one final chapter and one final P: Procreation.

# CHAPTER 7

# NEW LIFE

## JOSH

Chances are, if you're married, you've had at least one family member ask when you and your spouse will start having kids. While the time a couple takes before they start trying to conceive is different for everyone, it's a pretty common thing to see a couple get married, enjoy married life for a bit, and then begin starting their family. It's how the human race survives, after all! However, the topic of children can be a tough one for couples to talk about.

Those playful jabs from grandparents or well-meaning friends asking a married couple when they'll start having kids might seem harmless, but those words can cut like a knife to some. More specifically, asking (especially when it turns to nagging) a couple about their plans for kids is really something we should do with extreme care—or not embark upon at all if the person you're speaking with is only a casual acquaintance.

Why? Because the question of kids can expose a significant amount of heartache. A staggering number of couples struggle with infertility and find themselves walking through months and years of negative pregnancy tests, confusing and frightening doctors' visits, painful and expensive fertility treatments, and can often still not be able to conceive. Beyond a struggle to conceive, there are so many couples who have experienced the pain of a miscarriage, stillbirth, or the death of their child shortly after birth. It's a painful journey that often feels very lonely, scary, and confusing. And it seems to be only recently that couples have started being more open with their stories of infertility, miscarriage, and stillbirth. Because of that, it can sometimes feel as though you're the only person in the world experiencing such heartache, when it couldn't be further from the truth. Unfortunately, those who haven't walked through that particular journey can often unintentionally ask incredibly hurtful questions, such as, "When are you going to start having kids?" or "When are you going to give this little one a sibling?" These questions can feel like salt being rubbed into a wound and make everything feel worse and even more isolating.

If that is you, please know that you are not alone. If you and your spouse are dealing with infertility, miscarriage, or any other complication that is keeping you from starting your family the way you always dreamed, remember that you aren't alone and you aren't broken. There are so many other couples fighting through the same thing, and so many out there ready to link arms with you, walk with you, cry with you, pray with you, and one day celebrate with you. If you haven't had to endure that yourself, do your best to reach out to those brothers and sisters in Christ and support them as they navigate this complicated journey.

God is telling a beautiful story through the sexual union, but we must remember that we live in a fallen world where there is pain, heartbreak, and disappointment. Unfortunately, that means a lot of couples who want more than anything to conceive and have a biological child of their own will not be able to. Chances are, if you are standing in a group of married couples, there will likely be at least one (but likely more) couple who has walked through infertility struggles, miscarriage, or a stillbirth.

Those moments of yet another negative pregnancy test, the fear when a woman starts noticing that she's bleeding and having cramps during pregnancy, or the devastation when a woman hasn't felt her baby move for a long time, are very real and unfortunately all-too-common occurrences for couples trying to start their families. So while we need to be sure we keep those in mind and handle our brothers and sisters in Christ with care when we talk about families and having children, it doesn't mean that God's story of sex is destroyed or broken. Even more wonderfully, it doesn't mean that God can't and won't bring forth life through your marriage.

## SO THAT THEY MAY HAVE LIFE

I remember the wintery day in Chicago like it was yesterday. My wife and I had moved there so I could serve as the pastor of a church. We were far from home, we didn't know many people, we were cold, and my wife was pregnant. Typically, I attended every single doctors' appointment with my wife when she was pregnant with our son and also with this pregnancy, but it was the day before service, there were only three of us to clean out the church, and I still had a lot to do to get ready. So my wife told me to stay at the church and she'd go to the appointment alone. She said she felt as though something was going on, but she was totally fine seeing her doctor solo that day. Of course, when she drove back to the church, as soon as she got out of the car, I could tell by the look on her face that something bad happened, and I instantly started kicking myself that I hadn't been there with her. My wife miscarried, and we began the slow, painful journey of mourning and healing, all while living in a cold place far from home and our loved ones.

I couldn't help but think why something like this would happen when we were in the middle of God's will. Both my wife and I knew that we were supposed to be in Chicago working for this church. And yet, we were walking through this awful pain away from our support system and away from a place that felt like home. In Judges 8:4, we see Gideon talking about how God called the Israelites to fight against the Midianites, and ultimately delivered victory to the Israelites. But they were exhausted. The verse says, "Gideon and his three hundred men, exhausted yet keeping up the pursuit, came up to the Jordan and crossed it." They were in the center of God's will, following the path He had set out for them, but it didn't mean it wasn't incredibly difficult. And that's how my wife and I felt in that season. It was devastating, it was heartbreaking, it was exhausting, but we kept up the pursuit of Christ. We kept following Him, because we knew He had a plan for our lives. Twelve months later, our daughter was born, and the joy we felt at her birth was only doubled from the amount of growth and closeness we felt to each other and Christ as we walked through the pain of that miscarriage. It doesn't negate the pain of that loss or make it unimportant, but as we walked through that pain, exhausted and devastated by the loss of that pregnancy, we trusted God, and He didn't lead us astray, even when it was hard.

We live in a broken world, and that means that in our lifetimes we'll experience pain, and we'll walk through things that feel unfair and unjust. This is certainly true when it comes to couples who feel they have "done everything right," those couples who feel as though they've been faithful to God, they've tried their hardest to live out God's better story of sex, and yet they still find themselves walking through situations of infertility, miscarriage, or stillbirth. It doesn't seem right, and it doesn't seem fair, and it can be easy to look to God and ask why He allows such pain. In those moments, it's important to remember we live in a fractured creation. So for those couples struggling to conceive or experiencing pregnancy or child loss, they've run right into one of the painful symptoms of our unwell Earth. This doesn't mean you've encountered evidence of God's powerlessness, carelessness, or cruelty. And it certainly doesn't mean that God still isn't going to bring life—and life to the fullest—because our God is a God who redeems and makes beauty from ashes. A couple who wants children might be heartbroken that they can't seem to have a "traditional" pregnancy to bring a child into the world, but they can find a lot of other great options for starting a family, such as surrogacy or welcoming babies, children, or teens into their home who have lost their families or need a safe place to live temporarily through adoption and foster care. But sometimes even that doesn't work, and it can feel as though you are missing out on the joy of the procreation pillar of God's better story for sex. But here's the thing: when we talk about the procreation pillar, we're not just talking about kids.

Of course, it isn't surprising to see that a married couple having children is a part of God's better story of sex. As mentioned before, our relationship with Christ, the sacrifice He made on the cross, and the new hope we have in Him aren't just things that are nice to think about—they're things that have literally given each of us new life.

However, when we think about marriage, that new life doesn't just start when the wife gets pregnant. Each and every one of us is a male or female image-bearer of God, so when two image-bearers get married, something amazing happens. In Genesis 2:24, it says, "That is why a man leaves his father and mother and is united to his wife, and they become one flesh." When a male and female image-bearer of Christ marry, they become one flesh. That moment when two become one is, on its own, the creation of new life.

When a couple gets married, not only do they physically come together in the sexual union, but their lives become intertwined. Many couples decide to share the same last name, they have a shared bank account, and suddenly all big life choices are made with their spouse—their ultimate partner in life—in mind. The way family finances are spent is something that gets decided together; what jobs are accepted or turned down is decided with the future of the couple and a potential family in mind; and the idea of picking up and moving across the country can even happen on a whim if both spouses are on board.

Getting married is more than just a beautiful ceremony. It's literally two people looking at their lives on their own and beginning a new life where their spouse's needs and desires are just as important as their own. It's very similar to what happens when we accept Christ's gift of salvation. We step away from our old life and begin living a life intertwined with Christ. Though we won't get to experience that ultimate oneness on this side of heaven, we, too, find ourselves with a new life when we say yes to Jesus, just like a new life begins when you say yes to marrying your spouse.

We serve a God who creates and a God who makes all things new. So it isn't surprising that in His story of sex, we see how the marriage union isn't just meant to bring forth literal new life; it brings forth figurative new life from the covenantal delight we experience. Sex isn't just procreative when it comes to conceiving a child; it brings the two together as one, bringing forth a new, beautiful creation, and it brings new life to the couple.

Of course, that can't take away the heartbreak you might be feeling if you're walking through a miscarriage, infertility, or stillbirth, but it doesn't mean that you don't get to experience the new life in God's better story of sex. In fact, experiencing this new life is something that we all get to experience—single people, couples who just don't want kids, couples who are unable to physically bear children, and couples with children.

While we love to tout Genesis 1:28 as a reason to have kids—and often make couples who can't have (or don't want) kids and single people feel a bit left out of the narrative—that decree basically mirrors what Jesus tells the church in Matthew 28: to go and "make disciples of all nations." Ultimately, God's better story of sex is the story of the new life we have in Christ. So when we talk about procreation in His story, it isn't in just the literal form of bearing children. We are called to promote life in both raising children and discipleship, and both are key, important pieces to bringing forth Christ's kingdom.

## GOD'S STORY

God is telling an amazing, life-giving story through sex and the sexual union. As male and female image-bearers of Christ, we get to live out the proclamation He made over us when Jesus died for our sins on the cross. He promises that we'll spend an eternity with Him and our sins are washed away. The protection we have in the covenant relationship of marriage mirrors that protection we experience in the covenant relationship we have with Christ. We experience covenantal delight and pleasure within the boundaries of marriage, just like we experience covenantal delight and pleasure in our relationship with God, which will only increase when we are with Him for eternity. Thanks to the work He did on the cross, we can mirror in our own lives the miracle of new life through coming together as a married couple, bringing children into the world, and being faithful disciples with those around us.

Our world has a narrative for sex, but God's story is much better. When we understand that God created sex as a proclamation for protection, pleasure, and procreation, we can begin to approach purity and sex in a healthier way. But there is still one more piece to this puzzle. The reality is, we all have wounds, but the good news is, healing and wholeness are actually possible. So in Part Three, we will get really practical and learn how we can restore and move forward toward freedom.

PART THREE

# GOD'S GIFT
# OF FREEDOM

# CHAPTER 8

# WHAT'S YOUR STORY?

## DAN

Parts One and Two were about exploring both the beauty and power in God's design for purity and His story of sex. It is such a beautiful story, but unfortunately, so many of us have heard a twisted version that distorts (or steals entirely) the beauty God intended for us. The harsh truth is, we live in a fallen world, so it's not surprising to see something God created get distorted by our unwell Earth. People make mistakes, people stray from the path God has set before them, people make bad choices, people listen to bad advice, and people sin. So even though there is this beautiful story from God, simply knowing about that story doesn't mean we'll be free from the brokenness that comes with this world—at least on this side of heaven.

Technology has zoomed forward by leaps and bounds in a very short time. For someone born in the late seventies and eighties, they have memories of when phones were landlines with answering machines attached, microwaves were a brand-new appliance, first-gen video games were created, and they went from playing single cassette tapes in a boom box to playing multiple CDs on a giant stereo in their bedroom. They probably also remember when their family got their first computer and explored the internet. They probably also remember when the internet changed from dial-up so you could talk on the phone and surf the web *at the same time*! Then came cell phones (and they were just phones), but quickly came cell phones with internet service (and the terror of accidentally pressing the internet button as you frantically tried to close it before you incurred outrageous data charges), and then their first iPod or MP3 player. They remember going from driving somewhere using verbal directions received from a friend and using a map to make sure the directions were correct, to printing out directions from Yahoo, then getting a GPS for the car, and now simply GPSing straight from their phone.

That's a lot of movement in the technological world, and for Gen Xers, millennials, and the older Gen Zers, those leaps happened in their formative years. For a person in their early to mid-thirties in 2020, they remember going from having analog access to information and entertainment to jumping into their teen years with access to AOL Instant Messenger, which gave them access to friends and strangers at the click of a button. Then in their later teen years they began exploring the world of MySpace, Xanga, YouTube, and LiveJournal where they could not only interact with people across the world but could share pictures, short videos, and their thoughts on a global online platform. And technology has continued to explode from there.

Obviously, there are a lot of amazing things that have come from the advent of technology and social media, but with the good has come a lot of bad. The internet has made pornographic material easier than ever to access, and despite a pornographic website's feeble attempts at keeping out visitors that are under the age of eighteen, it's not hard to bypass that and find sexually explicit and graphic material with a few clicks, regardless of one's age. According to the American Academy of Pediatrics, "American media is thought to be the most sexually suggestive in the Western Hemisphere. The average American adolescent will view nearly 14,000 sexual references per year."[5] While social media can bring people together, it's also made it easier than ever to strike up illicit relationships as well. From extramarital relationships to the more dangerous and nefarious relationships between an adult predator and a child or even a sex trafficker and a targeted victim, technology has made it even easier to fall into destructive material and people who are on the prowl.

But it's not just the rise in technology! Movies and television shows have normalized more gratuitous sex scenes, and the messages those movies and shows send to their viewers normalize topics like casual sex, commercialized sex, objectification of men and women, premarital sex, affairs, and divorce. Unsurprisingly, with so much content swirling around us that is accessible at the mere push of a button, it's not surprising that many people in both secular and sacred spaces alike find themselves dealing with the consequences of sexual brokenness. Worse yet, those struggling with sexual brokenness often come to the church feeling overcome with shame, that there is something wrong with them, or even that they are beyond Christ's redemption. This messaging can often push those individuals to secular spaces that perhaps don't have any real answers, but they feel more welcomed there than with the church crowd because they aren't pounding the person with messages of condemnation, shame, and hopelessness over their brokenness.

We talk a lot about imagining a world free from sexual brokenness, and while we won't experience that true and complete freedom in this life, we can experience freedom in Christ. However, if we're looking at our current or past struggles, whether they've come in the form of poor choices or from encounters of sexual abuse or harassment, and we look at them through the lens of shame, guilt, and fear, we are stopped from finding any freedom before we can even begin finding the freedom we have in Christ.

Or maybe your story is different. Maybe you haven't experienced anything you'd deem as "sexual brokenness." So when you look at those who do fit the description in your mind, you can't help but think, *I'm glad it's not me!* However, that pride is also a form of bondage that stops us from experiencing true freedom.

Here's the truth: we are all sexually broken. I am. You are. Every single one of us is. You might push back on this idea, saying that you've never had sex outside of marriage, but the reality is, our sexual wholeness isn't based solely on our actions. Wholeness and experiencing God's better story of sex in the exact way He intended also tied to our hearts and our minds. In Matthew 5:27–28 it says, "You have heard it was said, 'You shall not commit adultery.' But I tell you that anyone who looks at a woman lustfully has already committed adultery with her in his heart."

This is a wildly different message than we get from our culture. There's an unreleased track from an early Katy Perry album called "U Can Look But U Can't Touch"; the '80s glam metal band Poison also has a song called "Look But You Can't Touch"; the Black Eyed Peas song "My Humps" has a lyric that says, "You can look but you can't touch it"; and those are just a few examples. The messaging that gives people a free pass to look and lust after someone as long as they don't physically act on those impulses is everywhere—not just in music. It's the idea that it doesn't matter what happens internally; as long as those urges, desires, and generally unsavory ideas don't find their way into the physical realm, they don't count.

But that's not the way our God works. Of course, God is interested in what we do physically, but He's even more interested in what happens in our hearts. He's interested in our motivations behind what we do and what drives us internally. We're all born into sin, and whether we commit a sinful act that others can see, or we hide sinful desires or thoughts within ourselves, it's all sin that separates us from God. So it doesn't really matter what you've done or not done, each and every one of us is sexually broken because each and every one of us is broken and sinful.

That sounds like a hopeless statement, but it isn't! God doesn't leave us in that state of brokenness. Our God is one who redeems and restores. When we become followers of Christ, He takes on our sin and our brokenness—all of it—and it is paid for by His sacrifice on the cross. It's a key, foundational piece to being a Christ follower. We are broken and we can't become whole alone, so we fall at the feet of Jesus. That's why we kicked off this book by reframing the conversation of purity into that of a relationship, not an achievement. We don't save ourselves from anything; it's not our self-control or our strong family values that keep us in a state of sexual wholeness and purity. Our purity, our redemption, and our restoration come entirely from Christ. So facing our sexual brokenness means we must look to Christ, thereby encouraging and leading others to look to Christ for redemption as well.

## GOD'S STORY DISTORTED

In Part Two, we broke down God's better story of sex into four main categories that we call the Four Ps: Proclamation, Protection, Pleasure, and Procreation. And we've already touched on some ways that both the church and our culture at large have missed the mark. But now it is time to heal, and in order to heal, we need to dig a bit deeper on the ways we see God's story of sex distorted. Every single one of us is dealing with sexual brokenness, and we've all missed the mark when it comes to honoring God's intention for sex. So if we can break down the ways we've all fallen short and reasons we all need to be purified daily through Jesus Christ, it can not only help us in our daily lives, but it can also improve how we interact with our brothers and sisters in Christ. How? In the ways we hold them accountable, and the grace that we extend to one another when we miss the mark. In the previous chapters, we've briefly touched on ways that our culture and the church might distort God's story of sex. So in the next few chapters, we're going to really dive into how we're distorting God's story, our own sexual brokenness, and most importantly, how we can find healing and freedom in Christ.

Let's kick things off with Proclamation, the first of the 4 Ps that encapsulates the other three. It is, ultimately, the core concept of God's story of sex, which is the way God uses marriage and the sexual union to tell us of His love for His people, and the unity and oneness He wants us to experience with Him in eternity. His story proclaims that Christ died for our sins, and if we decide to follow Him, we get to spend eternity in unfettered fellowship, intimacy, and closeness with our Savior. It is through dating, getting engaged, marriage, consummating that marriage, and procreation that God uses the various stages of our life to show us the relational journey we are embarking upon with Him. Two image-bearers of Christ coming together in marriage and the sexual union helps us understand the oneness we will one day have with Jesus in heaven.

So what happens when it gets distorted? Unfortunately, we can see this proclamation distorted in both secular and sacred spaces. Secular spaces often tout the message that sex isn't a big deal, and the most important thing is instant gratification by chasing whatever feels good as long as everyone involved is a consenting adult. But in the sacred spaces, we see God's story erased and the morality behind a person's sexuality heightened.

Suddenly, Christ followers find themselves buckling under the enormous weight to protect their own purity and save themselves for marriage in fear of being ruined or damaged goods.

Of course, this flies in the face of everything Christ is proclaiming in His better story! The fact that we are all sexually broken, the fact that we all miss the mark in every aspect of our lives (including sex) is precisely why we need to focus on God's better story of sex. Luke 4:18 talks about how Jesus came to give sight to the blind, and James 4:4 uses pretty clear language when God's people are described as adulterous and that we have a natural inclination toward idolatry, disobedience, and rebellion against God's teaching.

Sex certainly isn't a casual thing, but it's also not the arbiter of a Christian's moral compass, because as the Bible makes very clear: we are broken and without hope without Jesus' death on the cross. As followers of Christ, we should be highlighting the fact that we are all broken and that we need a relationship with Him to constantly purify us and make us whole. When we devalue the meaning behind God's better story of sex to a set of rules and a test of moral fortitude, we distort God's story and lose sight of His intention just as quickly and easily as those in secular spaces do when they strip sex of its importance and meaning. After all, our collective need for redemption is a key part of God's story of sex.

However, it's not only in distorting the proclamation of God's better story that we see us lose sight of the true meaning and intention behind the sexual union. We can also distort His story when we lose sight of the covenant relationship intended for sex, something we discussed in the second P, protection. God's story says that sex is a covenantal identity, and out of that flows love, trust, joy, and faithfulness. However, when we remove the protective element of the covenant relationship of marriage intended for the sexual union, it turns sex into almost a transactional act to produce nothing more than momentary gratification. It turns sex into an act of taking, even if both parties fully consent to the activities, as each party in the sexual union are most concerned about doing what feels good in the moment.

I have always liked the analogy that compares sex to a fire. When you've got a fire in a fireplace, it's great. It's protected by the walls around it, it's cozy, and it's a wonderful thing to enjoy. However, if you were to take that same match that you used to light a fire in your fireplace and you dropped it in a dry forest, the results would be catastrophic. Because ultimately, it isn't the fire that is the inherent problem. It's the location. The same can be said of sex. Sex within the covenant of marriage is meant to create an inextricable bond and closeness. It's meant to make you feel safe, loved, and appreciated. But outside of the safety and protection God intended in the marriage union, it can be catastrophic and utterly heartbreaking.

Keeping sex within the covenant of marriage is meant to provide each party of the marriage with a sense of security and safety within that covenant. When you strip that protective element away, it's easy to turn sex into something that is meant to harm, abandon, neglect, or expose. And as we've previously touched on, that is the polar opposite of God's intention for sex. So as you navigate your own relationships and move forward with being a steward of your sexuality with the knowledge of God's better story, if you find yourself in a moment with your partner where you are considering moving your relationship into a sexual one without marriage, remember that analogy of fire, and blow out the match. Because when we follow God's story and God's intention, we can experience something beautiful, but when we ignore those guardrails and distort God's story of sex by ignoring the importance of marriage, we welcome that sexual brokenness into our lives and the pain and heartbreak that inevitably come with it.

In communities of Christ followers, while the message that sex is reserved for marriage is usually made quite clear, we still see "cleaned up" versions of sexual brokenness that distort the protection intended for the sexual union. From flirting to steal attention, objectifying thoughts, using sex to manipulate, taking from instead of connecting with your spouse, re-exposing survivors of trauma and sexual abuse to triggering stories in the name of sharing a testimony, and turning a marriage into a place of performance and striving instead of one of safety and intimacy—they all distort God's story and expose areas of sexual brokenness.

A similar thing happens when we see the third P, pleasure, get distorted. In our culture, pleasure becomes the main focus, and we are told to live by the mantra of "if it feels good, do it." And while that can be a pretty unhealthy philosophy for just about anything in life, sexual or not, it can sound really good when someone encourages you to live by that mantra. After all, chasing whatever feels good offers instant gratification, and it's easy to disguise that behavior by saying you're chasing happiness or trying to take better care of yourself. It's important to take care of yourself, but when we chase after fleeting happiness without paying attention to God's teachings and His guardrails for keeping us safe, that mindset can quickly spin out of control.

However, as we've seen with the other Ps, it isn't just secular space that distorts. Christians have also twisted the meaning behind the pleasure we find in God's better story of sex. The truth is that sex is meant to be between a husband and wife, and that union is meant to be one that brings pleasure. Unfortunately, churches have pushed so many fear and shame-based messages on sexuality and the sexual union (even when it happens within marriage) that a message of shame and embarrassment has come across when discussing the pleasure God gifted us in the sexual union. Or, on the flip side, we'll see churches massively oversell the pleasure a person will experience when they first lose their virginity or on their honeymoon as a reward for "good behavior." That messaging might seem harmless, but for a couple that struggles with intercourse, especially in those early days of marriage, those messages can leave them wondering what they did wrong to be punished with such a challenging sex life with their new spouse.

God created sex, and He created it to be pleasurable. It's not the biggest thing in life that we need to chase above everything else, but at the same time, it's okay to admit that sex brings pleasure—especially when it's experienced within the guardrails and boundaries set before us by God. We don't need to be ashamed of how God made us, nor do we need to let those instincts and urges dictate our lives (and that can be said for just about any base instinct and urge we humans experience).

Likewise, we don't need to tout sexual pleasure as some sort of lofty prize to be experienced as a reward for a virginity well protected, and if you and your spouse find yourself dealing with pain, awkwardness, confusion, or general discomfort and displeasure in your sexual relationship, it doesn't mean you've failed at anything. Keep lines of communication and trust open with your spouse (another reason the protection of covenantal marriage is so important, for when things don't quite go as planned), seek professional or medical help when needed, and come together to bring your concerns to Christ. Sometimes these things take time, understanding, and communication—and it has nothing to do with your holiness levels.

The final way we can break down the distortion of God's better story of sex comes with the fourth P, procreation. As we discussed earlier, procreation can refer to the new life a couple literally creates when they conceive a child together, but it can also refer to the new life they create coming together as one couple, or the new life created when ministering to new believers. Unfortunately, the church has a bad habit of overemphasizing the importance of the nuclear family and bearing children. Oftentimes, women are told their ultimate goal or most lofty calling is to become a wife and mother, or flippant comments about not truly understanding love until bearing a child are tossed about in casual conversation.

Understandably, this situation can create a lot of pain and isolation for believers who don't have kids. Single people are made to feel ostracized and incomplete (twice over, as they aren't married *and* don't have kids), couples who don't want children are made to feel selfish, and those couples who have struggled through miscarriage, stillbirth, or infertility experience someone tossing salt into a deep, painful wound in a community of believers who are supposed to hold them up in this tough time.

It's why we wanted to be clear that procreation in God's better story of sex isn't just about children. Because your ability to understand God's love for His Church and to experience the amazing love of our Savior doesn't hinge on your desire for parenthood, functioning reproductive organs, or finding a spouse in your childbearing years.

But where the church exalts the family and bearing children to unhealthy high levels, we see bearing children vastly undervalued in secular spaces. We see the continued disdain for the life that springs from the sexual union in the ongoing struggle against abortion, but it doesn't just end there. Our culture also is one where having one or two absent parents isn't necessarily a rarity, and the responsibilities of bringing a child into the world are often disregarded in the form of men abandoning their partners during or after the pregnancy.

Having children (and a spouse) isn't the highest calling for a person, but it also isn't something a person can just shrug off either. Procreation stemming from the sexual union isn't just a wonderful outcome of sex, but it's also a responsibility that needs to be lived up to. And when we distort the procreative element of God's story of sex by either diminishing the importance and seriousness of a child resulting from the sexual union, or we tout the message that nothing is more important than having babies, we're missing the point of God's better story of sex. God is a God of creation and new life, and He is a God of redemption. It's why we get to experience that procreative element in literal terms of bringing forth children, but also in our relationship with our spouse, the way we create in the world as we follow God's plan for our lives, and as we build community and bring forward new believers.

The point of walking through these ways we can distort God's story of sex is to drive home a really important point: that each and every one of us has missed the mark. We've all messed up and distorted God's story of sex in our own lives (and potentially in the lives of others). It also helps us change our perspective moving forward. Instead of thinking about something regarding the sexual union and if it would be accepted in our church or our culture, we need to reframe our thinking to ask, "Does this proclaim God's story of sex?" Are our actions and thoughts supporting the story God is telling about His adulterous Bride, His amazing redemption and salvation, and our eternity with Him? Because if they aren't, regardless of how "bad" we might perceive our actions, or if we think it's not a big deal because what happens in our heads and hearts doesn't count, we're actively distorting God's story.

It's a blunt way to put that, and it can be hard to hear—especially for those of us who are guilty of looking down on our brothers and sisters in Christ for their own brokenness. The good news is, the story doesn't end there. We've all got sexual brokenness that we must take to the foot of the cross, but our gracious God takes that brokenness and makes us whole again.

The tricky thing is how we can responsibly address sexual sin and sexual brokenness in our own lives and the lives of those in our close community. That is, how can we hold those we love (and ourselves) accountable without hurling insults and shame at them? The first step is understanding and admitting that we all have sexual brokenness to sort through with Christ. If we can "remove the plank from our own eye" before holding our brothers and sisters in Christ accountable, we can come to them in a position of grace, love, and support rather than making them feel attacked, alone, and ashamed.

This world is broken, which means you and I are too. However, we believe there is hope for healing. In the next chapter, we will dive into the first way to go about finding the freedom, healing, and wholeness we are all searching for.

# CHAPTER 9

# PRAYER IS PROXIMITY

## JOSH

One of the hardest things about being a Christ follower is holding ourselves and those in our community accountable for their actions. At its core, accountability is quite a delicate needle to thread, and unfortunately (whether it is true for your specific community or not) the church doesn't have a great reputation when it comes to being a grace-filled place for sinners to come and find redemption. Sure, we do a great job when it comes to sharing about Christ's love, but so many people currently attending churches around the globe, and those who have sworn off any form of organized religion, have a story or two where a church made them feel unwelcome and unworthy because of their past. Oftentimes, when those poor decisions have resulted in a sexual sin, churches have a reputation of responding with an extra level of coldness.

Mercifully, this isn't true everywhere, but as we said in the very beginning of this book, a world free from sexual brokenness begins with you and me. So it's up to each and every one of us to start creating communities of believers who tell God's story of sex and address the sexual brokenness that we all have with grace and love. The enemy wants us all to continue living in a state of fear and shame, because it keeps us from the wholeness Jesus can give. It's our job as Christ followers to address our own sexual sin and encourage those in our community to address their own sexual sin while also remembering the freedom we have in Jesus' death on the cross.

God gave us the Holy Spirit to transform our behaviors and our hearts, so just as we aren't meant to "save ourselves" to maintain our purity, we're also not meant to "fix" our sexual brokenness. It's our job to admit it and take our sin to the cross. But what does that look like in practice? In this chapter, I want to give you one really practical way to start.

## EXPECTATIONS AND EMPATHY

When you think about someone addressing sexual sin in their community, what are your expectations? For some, it might be the equivalent of what happens to Hester Prynne in *The Scarlet Letter*, where she's forced to wear a red A on her chest as a public marker of shame after her Puritan community found her guilty of adultery. You probably aren't worried that your community will make you wear a literal badge to announce your sexual brokenness to your community and keep you firmly planted in an ever-deepening pit of shame. Fortunately, in most cultures today, we don't shame people in such an explicit way. Unfortunately, the shaming still exists in more implicit ways. Chances are, you're afraid you'll be eternally labeled as broken, disgusting, easy, or several far worse monikers.

On the flip side, especially when the sexual sin concerns a person in power abusing their rank to abuse, harass, or rape someone in their community, your expectations might be that the sin will be swept under the rug and the abuser will keep their position of power. Worse still, if you're the survivor of the abuse, you might fear that the blame will somehow be shifted to you, or you'll be made to feel at least somewhat responsible for what happened to you.

In either case, these reactions to sexual sin don't create communities based on love and grace. At best, these responses are based on perfectionism and performative Christianity rather than truly seeking to follow Christ's teachings and allowing Him to make us more like Him every day. At worst, it creates communities that claim to follow Jesus while using His name to protect abusers and make sinners in need of Christ's saving grace—which, for those keeping score at home, is all of us—feel too broken or too far gone to save.

So what do we do? How should we, as followers of Jesus, address sexual sin? As with everything we do, we must first look to Jesus. Grab your Bible and open it to John chapter eight. The chapter kicks off when Jesus is confronted at the temple courts by teachers of the law and Pharisees who were condemning a woman caught in adultery. They bring the woman to Jesus and ask what He thinks they should do, citing the law of Moses, which says she should be stoned.

Instead of picking up a rock, Jesus says in John 8:7 to the angry accusers, "Let any one of you who is without sin be the first to throw a stone at her." One by one, the accusers left, and when it was just Jesus and the woman, He said, "Woman, where are they? Has no one condemned you?" (v. 10). The woman looks around and says no one has. And it's in Jesus' next response when things get wild. Jesus, the sinless Lamb of God who would soon be crucified on a cross for the sins of the world, says to this woman who was *caught in the act* of adultery, "Then neither do I condemn you."

And He doesn't stop there. He offers her grace and forgiveness, but then says, "Go now and leave your life of sin."

Here's why that's such a revolutionary, expectation-subverting response. As the people who brought this woman to Jesus said, the response to this woman's sin, according to the law, was to kill her—stone her, specifically. It's a horrific, cruel, and slow way to kill someone. It's a punishment that really makes the accused wallow in their position and subjugates them to fear, humiliation, and incredible pain before ultimately snuffing out their life. The woman was caught actively engaging in adultery, so according to the law, it was a pretty open and shut case. She did the crime, and she needed to pay the price.

But amazingly, that's not how Jesus works. He came to Earth not only to bring salvation but to completely turn on its head the way we all think of justice. When presented with someone who had very clearly sinned—someone who had blown past the guardrails set before her by God—Jesus didn't side with the self-righteous accusers. Instead, He sided with the sinner. He showed love, and He showed mercy. Jesus, the One who always sides with the sinner over the self-righteous, led with grace. The Bible makes it clear that this woman wasn't being falsely accused. She was caught in the act and deserved to be punished. However, Jesus showed her grace, He showed her love, and He showed her the acceptance she hadn't gotten before. By doing that, He built the foundation of a relationship with that woman based on love and grace.

However, this interaction in John doesn't just speak to how Jesus defies expectation. It also shows His empathy. When approached by the woman and her accusers, the Bible notes something kind of weird. Jesus crouches and starts writing something in the dirt. Who knows what He was writing—the Bible doesn't say if He was just absentmindedly scribbling or if He was writing something specific—but it does show us a few things about how Jesus reacts to us when we sin. In that moment, Jesus didn't puff out His chest, He didn't raise His voice, He didn't shoot a withering glare at the woman, He didn't make a snide comment about her, and He didn't go on about how gracious He was about to be toward someone so clearly awful. Instead, Jesus crouched down and scribbled in the dirt.

Lots of ink and sermon space have been spent thinking about what Jesus wrote, but I think the real power is found in His physical stature in that moment. His posture is the point. When approached by someone found in sin, Jesus didn't puff Himself up—He got low. That woman, likely terrified and ashamed, was made to stand surrounded by a thrall of sneering accusers ready to take her life in a horrific fashion. Think of the body language of an accuser or an attacker. They make themselves as big as possible, as loud as possible, as powerful as possible. Why? To make their victim feel as small as possible, and to let that person know who is in charge in that interaction. Jesus didn't do that. He got low. Chances are, they probably made eye contact when He crouched down. It's certainly a possibility that He wrote something mind-blowing in the dirt, but to that woman, the really mind-blowing thing happened when He took on the physical body language to say, "I'm right here with you, and you're not alone."

He showed her grace, love, and acceptance in both His words and His body language. He made her feel safe, and He made sure she knew she wasn't alone. She was guilty. She knew it, her accusers knew it, Jesus knew it, everyone knew it. But to our amazing Savior, her story wasn't over. He defied expectations by pardoning her and, at the same time, stirred up conviction within her accusers. The amazing empathy He showed her—in what might have been the most terrifying moment of her life—created a life-changing relational foundation of love, trust, grace, forgiveness, and hope.

But that doesn't mean He just gave her a wink and a nod and said, "It's cool; don't worry about it." No, Jesus showed her love and forgiveness, and then hit her with some truth. He let her know He loved her, He let her know she was safe with Him, and He let her know that He wanted to have that relationship with her, and then He offered the truth she needed to hear to live out the story He had planned for her: "Go now and leave your life of sin" (John 8:11).

When confronted with sexual sin, Jesus led with love and grace. He led with empathy, and He led with an attitude that let His daughter know she was safe with Him. He made it clear that her worth wasn't marred or changed by her actions. He forgave her, and then He challenged her to do better. Did that woman sin again? Unless she died moments after that interaction, the answer is probably a resounding yes. Jesus wasn't calling her to be perfect. He was calling her to leave her life of sin and to follow the life He had for her.

It's that attitude—that grace-filled response to both sexual sin and sin in general—that we as Christ followers need to carry into our communities and churches. We must turn our communities into a place that has a relational foundation built on love and security and the grace we all have received from our Jesus. From there, we can defy expectations by responding to the sexual brokenness of those in our community with that grace, love, and empathy we saw Jesus extend to the woman in John 8.

## ADDRESSING SEXUAL SIN

So how can we address sexual sin in ourselves and our community in a real, effective way? What does Jesus' example in John 8 tell us? The first thing we must understand is, we are all vulnerable to sexual sin. It's human nature to think, *I might be a sinner, but at least I didn't do what* that guy *did*. And unfortunately, that sin-ranking system seems to take particular hold when it comes to the realm of sexual sin. While at first glance it might seem that this sort of thinking only hurts others in our community, it is a thought process that can inflict a lot of pain and shame on ourselves as well. A person who might present him or herself in their community as a beacon of sexual purity might struggle with a sexual sin they are incredibly ashamed of behind closed doors. And the very ranking system of sexual sins that this person has touted in public could be the very thing keeping them in the dark, hiding their brokenness, not willing to reach out to their community and receiving Jesus' offer of forgiveness and redemption.

If we can start from a place of understanding that we all have sinned and that we all have and will struggle with sexual brokenness, it can help us start from a place of empathy. It will also help us to understand that we all have been and will be tempted, and that temptation in itself isn't sinful (after all, Jesus Himself was tempted). However, it's how we respond to that temptation that matters. Whether we struggle with consuming sexually explicit content, keeping the sexual union within the boundary of marriage, having lustful desires, or something else entirely, when we understand that we all have fallen short, we all have sinned, and we all experience temptation, it can help us create a community of believers who are more empathetic and safer for those who are seeking Christ's freedom and forgiveness.

## THE PURE LIFESTYLE

The biggest thing when addressing sexual sin and brokenness is not to fall into a cycle of repeating the behavior. Don't let hang-ups turn into harmful habits. So in addition to creating a community where each person feels safe and loved when they are honest about their struggles, it's important to make a plan for how to, as Jesus put it, "leave your life of sin." Sexual sin can often be cyclical in our lives, so what we need is a new framework—a healthy lifestyle. That's why we've created something we call the PURE Lifestyle. Getting caught in this healthy loop will help us address sexual temptation as it comes into our life.

## P: PRAY

The first step is prayer. Prayer is undoubtedly the most powerful thing you can do. It is a key component in growing your relationship with Christ. Staying in constant communication with Him is proximity to the One who is pure and the best way to get to the core of what is going on in your heart. Spending time in prayer, asking God to reveal the root of sexual sin you struggle with and the ways you've been vulnerable to sexual temptation can not only help you be honest with yourself, but it can help you reset. After all, how can you expect to correct a problem if you've not properly identified what the problem is? It's why it's key to spend time in communication with God in prayer. Ask God to reveal where you've sinned, ask Him to let you know those places where you're vulnerable to temptation, and repent where you need to. He will hear you and help you.

## U: UNDERSTAND

This is where things get a bit more real. Understanding flows from intimacy with Christ. Once God has revealed the core of your sin, it's time to address those harmful and addictive behaviors connected to those sexual sins and temptations. If you struggle with consuming explicit content, it's vital to look at those addictive and harmful behaviors that draw you toward seeking out that content. If you're cheating on your spouse, what are the behaviors that repel you away from your partner? If you're engaging in casual sex, pinpoint what makes you engage in that behavior. But more than just understanding where you're falling from the path God has for you, it's also important to understand God's story and understand what He has for you.

First and foremost, you are a child of God. He created you in His image, male or female, son or daughter. Think about what help you need to stop that addictive and/or harmful behavior, and begin to learn and truly see the incredible plan God has for your life. Do you need a trusted friend to help you change your habits? Or maybe you need to seek help from a licensed therapist, a mentor, or a support group. Understanding your needs means taking a deep look at yourself and acknowledging where you're falling short. But remember this, God has set you apart as His child. You are fearfully and wonderfully made.

## R: RESOLVE

Once you've got a firm grasp on your own sexual brokenness, your temptations, and you've spent time understanding what's going on in your heart and God's story for you, it's time to make some changes. Just understanding a problem doesn't fix it, even if you tell lots of other people about your struggles. So once you've done the work to wrap your arms around what's going on, resolve to the fact that you can't do anything on your own and you must submit to God's greater plan and story for you. It's time to commit to submitting to God's story of sex. It's making the commitment to yourself, your community, and to God to turn away from those activities, thoughts, people, and other temptations that have kept you in this cycle of sin. It's time to resolve that you can't do this on your own. You must die to yourself daily—sometimes several times a day—and commit your ways to Him. Step away from those things that harm you and step into the grace and freedom we have in Christ. Begin walking in the fullness He has for you.

## E: ENGAGE

The final piece of the PURE Lifestyle is to engage. Don't just say that you're stepping away from those thoughts, activities, and social situations that cause you to engage in sexual sin. Find ways that you can really commit to your resolution and begin engaging in your new behavior. Add ways to be held accountable to your resolution. Remember, you aren't alone and you can't do this on your own. Rely on God and embrace His correction and guidance in your life. What that looks like will be a bit different for every person. But find a way to engage with someone in your community who will hold you accountable when you miss the mark while, at the same time, encouraging you to stay the course and keep following Christ's lead. That can look like adding some monitoring and blocking software onto your devices; it could mean seeing a counselor, a therapist, or joining a support group; or it could mean setting up an accountability relationship with a friend or mentor. You are the only one who knows what you need and what will help you make the right call when faced with temptation. But the important thing is to engage with the issue and make a plan with someone to help you from falling back into old habits.

## I'M NOT HURTING ANYONE

One of the toughest things about addressing sexual sin both in our communities and within ourselves is that oftentimes people have a different idea of what constitutes a sexual sin that is worth mentioning. Obviously, some people will have differing ideas on what is right or wrong, but sometimes it can extend beyond that, and the behavior can go unaddressed because the person committing the sin or someone around them thinks, *It's not that bad.*

This idea ultimately goes back to distorting God's story of sex and the proclamation that He is making through His story. If your actions, words, or the content you are consuming are subverting the proclamation of God's story of sex, if it's cheapening or twisting the narrative, it's a bigger deal than you think. This means it is something you need to take the time to bring to God in order to examine and work it out of your life. Even if you admit your actions, words, or the content you're consuming aren't great— or are downright wrong—but you keep it up (or don't call out a friend for it) because you're not impacting anyone but yourself, you need to do the same thing. Take that behavior, those thoughts, and that temptation to the foot of the cross.

The reality is, your actions have ripple effects within your community and the world at large. There are obviously some biological and natural consequences that can come with sexual brokenness, such as sexually transmitted infections, unplanned pregnancies, abortions, broken families, and broken hearts. Your actions never truly impact only you, even if those natural consequences can't or won't result from the sexual sin you struggle with. For instance, if you watch a lot of explicit television shows, watch pornography, or find other illicit content online, you're creating a demand or marketplace. We've all heard the phrase "sex sells," and it is unfortunately very true. When you spend your money to watch that show or that movie with the graphic nudity, you're sending Hollywood executives a message: "More of this, please!" When you get pornography online or download illicit pictures, you're telling those individuals that there is a market for that content, and you want them to create more. Wherever there is demand, there will be supply.

It's no secret that alongside sex workers who willingly participate in pornography, stripping, or prostitution—and the even more horrifying corners that engage in sex trafficking and exploiting minors—there are those who do that line of work out of desperation for money and limited options. And while you yourself might not be taking part in that illegal and nefarious stuff, your subscription, your purchases, and your downloads help that industry grow. At the very least, your decisions make this content more accessible to everyone (including minors); and at the very worst, they make the industry more capable of exploiting others.

However, stepping away from sexual sin (even when your actions don't directly hurt someone) isn't just about this slippery slope or this ripple effect. When you excuse or justify sexual sin as not hurting anyone, you're ignoring the one person you're hurting the most: yourself. As we've mentioned before, admitting your own sexual sin and walking in the freedom we all have because of Jesus' grace are key to living your life to the fullness that He wants. God has amazing plans for you, and you can't fully walk forward in freedom if you're bound and held back by your own actions.

Obviously, even the most ardent Christian is going to sin regularly—it's a part of being a human in our fallen world. However, if we fail to look at our sin as sin, and we fail to bring that sin to Jesus and seek forgiveness and wholeness, we're allowing something to stand between us and Christ, which means separation. It won't steal our salvation from us, and it won't stop our God from loving us, but it will hinder us from experiencing intimacy with Him and everything He's got for us in this life. And, by extension, it will mean that we won't fully experience the life He intended or touch the lives He intended for us to touch. To be clear, it doesn't mean that our actions can muddle God's plans, but if we're not in a place where we can be the hands and feet of God in a situation, He'll call someone else to fill that role.

God's plans for us and this world are intricate and amazing, and when we let ourselves stay trapped in sexual sin, we're actively putting blocks between us and the plans God has for us. And at its core, it's one of the big problems of "ranking" sexual sins. If you excuse your own behavior because it isn't that bad or it isn't hurting anyone, or if you allow sexual sin to continue in your community because it's not as bad as other stories you've heard, you're allowing each person involved to actively put up barriers between themselves and God. And by fostering that ranking system in your heart or letting it take root in your community, you're creating a space that cannot experience the grace, love, empathy, and forgiveness that we see Jesus extend to the woman in John 8.

Our actions matter, our thoughts matter, and what's happening in our hearts matters. God cares about it all, regardless of how big or small the sin is. It's up to us to be honest with ourselves and one another, to have the grace and love and forgiveness that Jesus modeled, and to address sexual brokenness and sexual sin when we see it and not let it slide by. Stop getting caught in the same old cycles of sexual sin, and start getting caught up in a healthier life—the PURE Lifestyle!

# CHAPTER 10

# YOUR PAST DOESN'T DEFINE YOU

## DAN

One of the most harmful messages that purity culture has perpetuated about sexual sin (or even worse, being the victim of sexual assault or rape) is that a person can be "damaged goods" based on what sexual activity they have engaged in. It's such a harmful message because it's about as far from what the gospel teaches as anything can be. Jesus came to Earth to spread a message of redemption, love, and hope. He's a God who offers second chances, forgiveness, and wholeness. And yet, we've allowed ourselves to believe that our sexual brokenness makes us damaged goods. Nothing could be further from the truth, but too many of us walk around feeling less in the eyes of our community, future (or current) spouse, and God Himself.

We see this dangerous belief played out in so many different ways, but there is one particular story that has always stuck out to me. During one of our events, a thirteen-year-old girl approached me and let me know she had been raped when she was just eight years old. That story alone is a harrowing one, but what she said next utterly broke my heart. She told me that people at her church told her she could never be pure again because her purity was taken from her when she was raped. The core message of purity culture—the idea that we are to "save ourselves"—wasn't even an option for this girl. Someone else took making that decision from her, and, according to the lies her church was perpetuating, she didn't just lose her innocence and sense of safety when she was raped, but also her purity was irrevocably stolen from her. Eight years old and she was already irredeemable, damaged goods.

Unfortunately, this girl's story isn't a rare one. Fourteen-year-old Elizabeth Smart was asleep in her bed one night when a man entered her room and kidnapped her. For the next nine months, Elizabeth was held captive and traveled with her captor while being sexually assaulted and raped numerous times. Happily, Elizabeth was rescued and returned to her family, and she now uses her voice to advocate for other victims of sexual assault. But even now as a woman in her thirties with a husband and children, she has still said on multiple occasions that she was embarrassed to tell her parents that she was repeatedly raped while she was kidnapped. Worse yet, she feared that because of what her captor did to her, her purity was as destroyed as a "chewed up piece of gum," as she had been taught in her church.

The good news is, Elizabeth Smart's case was a widely publicized one, and she's had lots of advocates around her to shut that misconception down. In the case of the thirteen-year-old girl we met at our pureHOPE event, I was able to speak the truth about God's love, Christ's redemption, and the truth of what purity truly is and the amazing work Jesus does in our lives to make each of us new every day. Had God not ordained my meeting with that girl, how differently might she have moved through her life?

Where would her life take her as she moved through the years believing she was broken, unfixable, and damaged goods? And now that she knows the truth, now that she knows about her worth and identity as a child of God and the amazing redemption and daily renewal we find in our relationship with Jesus, how much more hopeful are things for her? Now she can look ahead with the security she is meant to have in her true identity and the peace that her past doesn't define her. Now the only one who has any say in her identity is Jesus—the One who died on the cross for her, and the One who spends every day making all of His children new.

However, there are so many of us, maybe even some of you who are reading this book, who haven't heard this message of truth until now. Instead, you've spent years under the weight of being labeled as damaged goods because your purity was either stolen from you or it's been irrevocably damaged because of choices you've made. Worse yet, maybe you're like that thirteen-year-old girl and had your ability to choose what you did with your body taken from you. Not only are you wrestling with the lies that you're permanently marred by that event, but you've also been fed lies that you could have prevented the violence if you hadn't done something, worn something, drunk something, said something, or been somewhere that "allowed" your rape to happen. It's easy to take on shame because you think you could (or should) have done something to stop or prevent the attack.

So before we say anything more, let's make this abundantly clear: *you're not damaged goods.* If you're a rape or sexual assault survivor, you weren't attacked because you weren't holy, pure, or smart enough to stop it. Most importantly—and this goes for both survivors and people who have done things in their past they aren't proud of—you're not beyond repair or too broken to fix. You're not too far gone for Christ's renewal and redemption to reach you. Do sexual sin and sexual brokenness leave a mark? Yes, absolutely, and sometimes those consequences can follow you for the rest of your life. Trauma can leave deep wounds, especially when it occurs during childhood or from a person you trusted. However, that doesn't mean you can't experience freedom and redemption, and it doesn't mean you don't get to heal from your past. Your past might have left a mark, but the amazing news is, we serve a God who cares and who heals!

Healing from sexual brokenness is just like any other form of healing—it takes time. The bonds that keep us in our sexual brokenness and sexual sin have likely built up over the course of a lifetime. As we said, sexual sin tends to happen in a cyclical nature in our lives. You can't undo the damage overnight. And as frustrating as it might be to hear, healing isn't always linear; you're going to have setbacks.

This is true for any sort of healing. Paul himself says in Romans 7:15: "I do not understand what I do. For what I want to do, I do not do, but what I hate I do." Of course, with the stigma surrounding sexual brokenness and sexual sin, setbacks in healing from those areas can feel extra frustrating. However, we've got to realize that when we engage in a lifelong pursuit of purity, it means exactly that: a *lifelong* pursuit. It means we're going to have seasons when we are on top of the world, and when we feel very close to the Lord and so proud of how far we've come. But we'll also have seasons when we have setbacks. We'll mess up. We'll stray from God's teachings. We'll make a bad decision. We'll fall back into old habits.

While that can feel incredibly frustrating, it's important that we realize the truth of the matter: while we're all broken, we've been made whole in Christ! So even though it's disheartening and frustrating when we do what we hate, as Paul says, we must remember that Jesus is right there, purifying us. We only need to take our sins to Him on the cross and continue letting

Christ do His work in us. Even though we're going to mess up, we must keep moving forward and claiming the victory we have in Him.

Letting sin from our past define us is one of the best ways the enemy can contort the truth about our identity in Christ and stop us from living the life God has for us. Here's a truth we've mentioned briefly in the book, but the reality of it should hit a bit differently now: our brokenness, our sin, and our need for forgiveness and redemption are 100 percent vital parts of God's story of sex. We've mentioned before that the church is frequently called the adulterous Bride of Christ, and our brokenness and the fact that we will sin—we will miss the mark—until our final day on this earth is precisely why. God knows we're living in a fallen world, and He knows that we are fallen creatures. Not only does He not expect perfection from His children, but He uses our failures to show His amazing love and redemption. Not only can we never be too broken or too far gone for Jesus to save, but a key part in using our lives and the sexual union to tell the story of His love is that He's able to highlight how He makes all things new and how He can offer new life to us in the face of our failures.

While this is incredibly good news—and is a lifeline you can cling to when you find yourself feeling as though you can't find the way out of your own sin—it can be hard to know where to start. For example, perhaps you have the head knowledge that Jesus loves you and wants to redeem and restore you, but you don't know how to even begin finding your way to (or back to) Christ.

Here's what you need to know: not only does our God know that we will fall short, but He also knows that we will need Him to rescue us again and again. It's not up to us to find our way out of the pit we've dug ourselves into. Instead, we simply must cry out to our heavenly Father to rescue us. It's not about our power, our holiness, or any part of our efforts that will save us. Rather, it is fully submitting to God's power and the acts of Jesus Christ on the cross. So when we find ourselves in the midst of sexual sin, the first step to healing is simply acknowledging there is a problem and confessing it.

## CONFESS IT

The first step toward true healing is acknowledging the pain and talking about it. That might seem like a no-brainer, but this goes beyond simply saying, "I messed up, and I need help." This is about us owning up to the truth of our lives and our actions. Where the enemy has tried to keep you in darkness, in secrets, and silenced by your shame, it's important that your first step toward healing comes from shedding light on the dark and exposing all of your secrets. It's important to confess your sin to God, but it's also important to tell another trusted person in your life who can walk with you on the road to healing. If you're married, tell your spouse, but a mentor or close confidant are also great options to whom you can confess.

It's really hard to be so honest with another person because it makes you vulnerable, but as we've said many times before in this book, you and I are called to live in community. That means we need one another, and it's through holding one another up—and holding one another accountable—that we can grow and thrive in the life God has for us on this earth. While you might eventually get to the place where you feel comfortable being completely open with your past struggles with someone, don't feel as though you have to explain your struggles to all of your friends, family, and colleagues. Confessing to God, confessing to your spouse, confessing to a confidant is more than enough to engage in the healing process. Getting rid of those secret areas of shame doesn't have to mean telling the entire world about your weakest moments. It's more about being honest with your actions in the past and getting the earthly support you need to continue on your journey to healing.

## PURSUE INTIMACY WITH CHRIST

Acknowledging your brokenness is only the first step. Once you've done that, it's time to really dig in to why it's important to understand the reasons you made the choices you did, the intentions God has for you, and the power and importance that are found in God's better story of sex. If you really want to make a change for the better in your life, if you really want to follow Jesus' leading and experience that lifelong purification in your relationship with Him, you've got to spend time with Him. Actively pursuing intimacy with Christ is a vital part in seeking healing for sexual brokenness. An authentic and ever-deepening relationship with God isn't going to magically stop you from sinning, and it's not going to mean you'll never struggle with temptations or the sins from your past. However, when you spend time in the Word, when you spend time getting to know Jesus more, getting to understand His heart, and allowing Him to restore your heart, you change. Your desire to please Him overrides your desire to please yourself.

Pursuing healing from sexual brokenness isn't just an exercise in behavior modification. It's not about saying, "You did *that* before, now do *this*," over and over. Jesus isn't just interested in our actions; He's also interested in what's going on in our hearts. So when we pursue intimacy with Christ as we work to heal from our sexual brokenness, we're not asking Jesus to show us the right thing to do but the right things to think and believe. Though it isn't always the case, chances are, you likely know where you messed up, and you know what choices you should have made in many of your past encounters with sexual sin and brokenness. Intimacy with Christ and the purification we receive in our relationship with Him are a matter of working on heart-level transformation and a true renewal of our minds. We're not only learning what God calls us to do but why He calls us to those things. And when we begin to understand even a small part of the heart of God, ours changes too.

## TRUST THE PROCESS

A question you might be asking now is, "What does this have to do with healing?" When you break a bone, the healing process doesn't just center around healing the actual bone. The level of your injury and the time you spend in a cast and use crutches often mean you have to do some work—such as physical therapy—to restore the muscles surrounding that bone so it can support it when it's fully healed. The process can be painful, but you know you're working toward living a normal life again. It's also a time to evaluate whether you were doing something dangerous or unhealthy that led to the break, which may mean changing your habits so it doesn't happen again. Or you might learn that you've got a medical condition that makes your bones more susceptible to breaks, so not only do you have to heal, but you also have to understand your body's limitations for moving forward as injury free as possible. It's a similar idea with healing from sexual brokenness. You have to go through the process and trust in its results.

When we acknowledge our sin and come to the feet of Jesus to confess and seek forgiveness, the wrong is righted. Cast on, bone set, good as new. Jesus paid our debts on the cross—we just need to come to Him when we mess up and tell Him about it. Just as quickly as He forgave the woman caught in adultery in John 8, He'll forgive us too, and as it says in Psalm

103:12, "as far as the east is from the west, so far has he removed our transgressions from us." But it's up to us to then turn from our old ways and continue to seek intimacy with Christ to strengthen our hearts and our minds so we're equipped to avoid the same pitfalls. It's up to us to continue seeking the heart of God so He can transform ours. It's up to us to try to understand the story He is telling and why that story is so important. Then our actions not only change, but our hearts, minds, and our desires change. Without intimacy with Christ, without that heart-level transformation, any healing we seek for our sexual brokenness will just put a band-aid on a deep, gaping wound. It's when we pursue and find that intimacy—it's when we really do the heart work needed to let Christ transform our hearts and our minds—that we find ourselves not only healed but made new.

## SEEK WISE COUNSEL

As vital as intimacy with Christ is for healing, it doesn't mean that seeking help on Earth is pointless or a waste of time. In fact, sometimes seeking a professional to help you work through your sexual brokenness and your healing is vital for getting yourself out of the mire you feel trapped in and stepping into freedom. If addiction has sprung from your sexual brokenness, if you're processing through trauma, or if sexual brokenness has caused a serious rift in your marriage, it might be helpful to investigate your options with a professional.

If you've never seen a counselor or a therapist, it might feel weird or uncomfortable bringing a stranger into some of the most private areas of your life. However, seeking a licensed professional therapist or counselor—a Christian one, especially—can really help you unpack and process through your healing journey. As an objective third party, they can often see the larger picture a bit more clearly, help you identify problem areas you're not able to identify on your own, then help you make a plan to find your way out. Additionally, if your marriage has been threatened by sexual brokenness, an objective third party can also help you and your spouse communicate and heal more effectively than when you're both caught in the throes of intense emotions, such as shame, betrayal, and hurt.

Of course, seeking a licensed professional might not be the right fit for you. Sometimes group therapy or a support group can help you gain the perspective and objective help that you need. Sometimes counseling options at your church or with your pastor or trusted mentor can be enough. The point is, there are a lot of options out there to help you unpack your own sexual brokenness, where you are in the healing process, and where you hope to grow in the future. The Christian community can sometimes scoff at the idea of seeking professional help—it has been misconstrued as seeking the counsel of humans over the counsel of God. However, that perspective couldn't be more wrong. We weren't built to be in community just so we could have friends to hang out with on Friday nights and to watch our kids occasionally. The journey to freedom is not a solo trek. We need one another along the way. Community also means that those of us who are hurting and those of us who need help can find it. Seeking that help from a licensed therapist, a counselor, a support group, or a mentor isn't preferring humans to God as long as we're continuing to pursue intimacy with Christ—it's using the tools and the resources He has given us.

Leaning on community is a vital key to healing. Perhaps you don't find yourself in a place where counseling is necessary, and, if that's the case, it doesn't mean for a second that you're called to embark on your healing journey alone. We as humans are built to need others—we were created with an instinctual need to find "our people" and walk through life together. Followers of Jesus are hard-wired to find others seeking after the same Savior we are in order to link arms and embark on an honest journey together while fellowshipping and growing with other believers who want freedom in Christ.

This need for community is another amazing way God shows His grace and love for His children. Naturally, we see it in our relationship with Him, but we can also see how wonderful our God is in the way He uses His imperfect servants to come into our imperfect lives, build a relationship, and walk with us as we bring grace and truth to the sin in our lives. We can celebrate with one another and support each other through struggles and heartbreak. It is those imperfect servants—our community of fellow Christ followers—who walk alongside us and graciously help us confront those areas we might feel a reticence to face a problem. And they can support us and cheer us on as we embark on our journey of transformation and healing.

This is one great way to see God's better story playing out in our lives, regardless of marital status. A community of believers who find themselves under Christ's covenant, these fellow members of God's Church—the Bride of Christ—are one way we can experience His covenant protection and the procreative nature of a relationship with Jesus. New life develops when a body of Jesus followers gets together and walks through life together. There is protection found when you've got a community of brothers and sisters holding you up, watching your back, and calling you out in love when you've missed the mark. It's absolutely a picture of the protection we find in our covenant with Christ and the new life and joy we find as believers unlike ever before until we are in heaven with Jesus.

## I KNOW THE WAY OUT

On the television show *West Wing*, arguably a modern classic, one of the characters, Josh, finds himself spiraling out of control as he experiences intense PTSD after being shot. After Josh's behavior got increasingly troubling, his boss and unofficial mentor, Leo, orders Josh into therapy. When Leo approaches Josh after a session and asks how it went, Josh brushes him off initially but finally confesses that things have gotten so out of control he punched through a window in his apartment.

Without missing a beat, Leo shares a story that has become somewhat legendary for *West Wing* fans. He tells the story of a man walking down the street when he suddenly falls in a hole. The walls are so steep he can't get out, so he starts yelling for help from passersby. A doctor passes by, writes a prescription, tosses it in the hole, and moves on. A priest walks by, writes down a prayer, throws it in the hole, and walks on. Then a friend comes by, and when the man calls out, the friend jumps in the hole. The man in the hole yells at his friend, "Are you stupid? Now we're both down here!" But his friend says, "Yeah, but I've been here before, and I know the way out."

That story is such a great picture of why God has called us to live in community. Doctors and therapists can be vital as we process healing. Pastors or clergy people from our home church can also be vital in processing our pain and questions about God and our faith as we journey to healing. And as we've mentioned before, sometimes it can be vital to talk to someone who is an objective third party as we process pain, trauma, and brokenness. However, there is something truly special and unlike anything else: having friends around us to help us find the way out of the hole we've fallen into. Building an authentic community built on love and truthfulness means that we can call out to our friends unashamed when we find ourselves in that hole, and they'll jump down next to us and help show us the way out.

The enemy wants to keep us trapped in shame, isolation, and separation, but God has a life for us full of forgiveness, acceptance, and healing. And it's through community that we can not only heal and find support, but it gives us a group of people who can use their own moments from the pit and their own journeys of brokenness and healing to help us transform, heal, and find amazing freedom in Christ.

## WORTH THE EFFORT

One of the biggest lies we tell ourselves (and that the enemy feeds into) is that we're not worth the effort it will take to heal. Or perhaps that the journey will be too arduous, so we can do a few things here and there to heal, but we just don't have it in us to really put in the work. But that is a lie meant to keep us in bondage. It's a lie meant to hold us back, and that lie puts blinders on us that not only keep us from seeing the sprawling nature of God's plan for our own lives and all of His people, but it keeps us from seeing the reality that Jesus is right there, ready to walk through it all with us.

Healing takes work. Healing can be painful. Healing can be emotionally, spiritually, and even physically taxing. However, it is worth it because you and I are worth it. We aren't damaged goods, and our past doesn't define us. Just as Jesus told the woman in John 8 to go and leave her life of sin and she instantly found herself at a new beginning, Jesus is ready to do that for us. Whether you feel as though you've messed up in catastrophic ways or you're reconciling the idea that you struggle just as much with sexual brokenness as anyone else, Jesus is ready to forgive you and heal you.

Confess your sins to the people you trust, keep pursuing intimacy with God, and seek out wise counsel to help you put together a game plan. It's going to take some work, but *your freedom is worth the effort*!

Perhaps you've lost the plot of God's better story of sex, or perhaps you've been living in a way that is utterly antithetical to His story. Either way, you're worth the effort to seek healing and restoration. We say over and over that a world free from sexual brokenness starts with you and me. Obviously, our world won't ever be fully free until we step into eternity, but by seeking healing and wholeness within ourselves, we can become a vessel to help heal some of the brokenness in this world and help others to see the beautiful, powerful story that God is telling through sex.

What areas of sexual brokenness in this world would you like to see lose their grip on our society? Sexual abuse? Sexual shame? Struggles with lust? Worry for the next generation? We can help free people from that! But we can't if we are just as bound, just as trapped as they are. That's why we are writing this book. We want to hop down into the pit with you. We've been there before, and we know the way out, and we know what God thinks about you in the meantime. We serve a God who sees you as priceless and worth every second, every tear, and every ounce of effort it takes to find restoration from your sexual brokenness.

God is telling a beautiful story of His love for His Church through sex, and a part of that story is His love for His adulterous Bride. Your brokenness doesn't disqualify you—it reminds you that you are a part of the beautiful redemptive story. Your healing is a part of the plan. It means that you get to be a living example of God's amazing love and forgiveness, and it means that, if you're willing, you'll get to hop down and help someone else find their way out of the pit as well. Let's get rid of any messaging in our churches and communities that our sexual brokenness somehow makes us destroyed, beyond repair, or unwanted. Jesus wants us, and He's ready to restore us right now. We just have to reach out to Him and ask for His help.

# CHAPTER 11

# FEARFULLY AND WONDERFULLY MADE

## DAN

After understanding God's better story of sex, acknowledging our own sexual brokenness, and healing from our past, how do we move forward? What are we meant to do when it comes to living each day in the reality of God's better story of sex? While there are some things made explicitly clear in the Scriptures of what we should or should not do when it comes to sex—such as saving the sexual union for the covenant relationship of marriage—there are some things that aren't as clearly spelled out.

We've mentioned a bit of that strain between our culture and the church and the diametrically opposed messages we often find in sacred and secular spaces. Our culture prioritizes instant gratification and a carte blanche validation of all desires and interests, as long as all parties involved are willing participants. But God's better story of sex requires a bit more restraint from us, prioritizing the story God is telling over our instinctual desires. While it's always going to be a struggle not to act in the face of temptation, it can feel pretty easy to at least *identify* God's way when it comes to issues such as having an extramarital affair, having sex before marriage, or looking at and watching pornography. However, there are some things our culture has made a bit more unclear when it comes to identifying something that goes against God's better story of sex and purity.

As we stated earlier, once we understand God's story and have sought healing from our own past, we need to look at the world and the content we consume with a simple question: is this supporting or distorting God's story of sex? We know that pornography is something we should avoid. But what about television shows, movies, and music? Do we only need to avoid movies with explicit sex scenes? What about shows that have a sex scene but all parties involved are covered? What if there isn't an explicit sex scene but the entire movie or television show is about sex or losing your virginity before marriage? And while we're at it, what are the rules when it comes to music? Is there a specific age when it's okay to start listening to songs with sexual content? Does it matter if the song is crass in its reference to sex or if it uses a clever metaphor? What about the singer's costumes or dance moves?

Questions such as these can virtually drown you in feelings that there are too many rules and there is simply no way to be a human in the twenty-first century without consuming something that will distort God's story of sex, so there's no point in trying and it's not worth the effort in the first place.

But let's get out of the weeds and look at the larger picture for a moment. When we say the word "sex," typically someone is referring to the act of intercourse. However, sex isn't just about a physical act—it's also about identity, male and female. At the chromosomal level, we are all male or female image-bearers of God. The sexual union is about two image-bearers of Christ coming together in one of the most potent images of God's love for His children that we can get.

In Genesis 1:27, we see that we are all intentionally created to be male or female image-bearers of Christ: "So God created mankind in his own image, in the image of God he created them; male and female he created them." It's a short verse packed with power, explaining that God intentionally created us as men and women in His image. Additionally, it tells us our identity wasn't specifically chosen for our own purpose but also for pointing our identity directly back to God.

So what does that have to do with which movies you watch? It turns out, everything.

As image-bearers, our very being, our utter existence is designed to tell God's story. Everything we do as male and female image-bearers reflects (or doesn't reflect) God to others. That may feel like a weighty responsibility, because it is! Obviously, we're not always going to get it right, which is why we must foster our relationship with Jesus so we can be purified by Him every day and continue moving and working to becoming more like Him. However, this understanding that sex is about identity before it is ever about a physical act shakes up the story a bit. If purity is the pursuit of our relationship with Jesus and sex is ultimately about identity, it means that every part of our life, everything we do, everything we say, and every piece of content we consume matters, especially in contrast to what the world says and thinks.

It can feel easy to shrug off a movie, a show, or a song as though it's not a big deal. After all, the Ten Commandments doesn't say, "Thou Shalt Not Watch *Game of Thrones*." However, as we've said all along, a world free of sexual brokenness starts with each of us, and our actions always have a ripple effect. This means that we need to look at every aspect of our life not wondering if something is okay to do or watch, but we need to look at the larger picture and ask the question, does this help or hurt when it comes to my place in God's story of salvation, redemption, and His love for His Church?

If you're looking for a comprehensive list of shows, movies, and music that you shouldn't listen to, we're about to disappoint you. Because ultimately, it's not up to us to tell you what you should and shouldn't do, watch, or listen to. It's up to you to listen to what the Holy Spirit says to you as you grow closer to Jesus each day and as He continues to heal and purify your heart. If that sounds like a bit of a journey and a process, you're absolutely right! Our journey with Jesus is lifelong and filled with purifying and strengthening multistep processes. You're not going to wake up tomorrow and know exactly everything you should and shouldn't watch, and you're not going to suddenly be free from old temptations. It's a journey that will take time as Jesus and the Holy Spirit do their work in your heart to help guide you through sloughing off those old actions, thoughts, and desires that were keeping you in bondage.

The questions we should be asking have less to do with our actions and more to do with our identity and who we are in Christ. Every day, we must ask ourselves if our actions, thoughts, and the content we consume help or hurt our part in God's story. If our identity is rooted in being a male or female image-bearer of Christ, are we doing things that support that fact and point to God, or are we engaging in behaviors that distract from God's story and God's truth? Are we, intentionally or not, helping the enemy distort God's better story of sex? To better understand this, let's dive a bit deeper into our identity as image-bearers and how it plays into our lifelong pursuit of purity.

## NOT A MISTAKE

This might sound like a cliché, but you and I weren't made by mistake. Everything about us was planned by God well before we were born. He planned a world in which you and I would be His male or female image-bearers and the ways we might help bring the kingdom of God to Earth. As King David wrote, "You created my inmost being; you knit me together in my mother's womb. I praise you because I am fearfully and wonderfully made; your works are wonderful, I know that well. My frame was not hidden from you when I was made in the secret place, when I was woven together in the depths of the earth. You saw my unformed body; all the days ordained for me were written in your book before one of them came to be" (Psalm 139:13–16).

These verses tell us that not only are we "fearfully and wonderfully made," but our identity as a male or female image-bearer was something God planned out very intentionally for you and for me. He saw our unformed body and He ordained our identity, as well as each and every one of our days well before we were born. This describes our true identity, all the way down to a chromosomal level. We are each intentionally planned; no one is a mistake. So what does it mean to be a "real man" or a "real woman"? After all, there is often a lot of talk in both secular and sacred spaces about what that means.

Frankly, most of our definitions of "true" masculinity and femininity come from cultural norms and cultural expectations—meaning they change and evolve as our culture does. During WWII, masculinity centered largely around bravery and patriotism. That meant being willing to put oneself into the fight against fascism, not expressing fear, death, or pain, and not showing heartbreak while leaving one's family—often for years at a time. Women started joining the military as nurses, the Women's Army Corps, and images like Rosie the Riveter were used to encourage women to take up jobs in fields such as munitions and aircraft to help support life here on the home front. In that era, a "real" woman was rolling up her sleeves to either directly help the war efforts by joining the military or working stereotypical male-occupied spaces to keep the war effort and life at home going as smoothly as possible.

However, by the 1950s, the roles changed. For men, the role was to dress well, get a steady job, marry a nice girl, have kids, and raise a respectable family. A "real" man went from someone willing to throw his body in front of a bullet for the good of the country to someone who put on a nice suit every day, went to an office, climbed the corporate ladder, and had 2.5 children before he was thirty-five. Likewise, what made women truly feminine in our culture's eyes focused largely on homemaking. That meant not working outside the home, keeping the house running smoothly, having and raising children, cooking and cleaning, all while making sure she dressed smartly and kept herself made up for her husband (or potential husband). That was what made a woman a "real" woman back in those days.

And these are just *American* ideas of masculinity and femininity. Different countries and cultures also put differing levels of emphasis on behaviors, jobs, or familial structures that are masculine or feminine. People spend a lot of time wringing their hands because the behaviors, clothes, jobs, families, emotional maturity levels, and favorite pastimes constantly evolve in their attachment to a culture's idea of masculinity and femininity. If a man likes to cook, some laud it as a pastime hobby while others call it a "woman's job." If a woman works in a field such as carpentry, some praise her for her decision to embark into a male-dominated field, while others warn her that she's becoming too manly and will never find a husband.

So what does this mean for you and me? If we're called to be male or female image-bearers of Christ, does it mean we'll constantly need to restructure our identity to meet the new cultural norms of masculinity and femininity to be sure we're as masculine or feminine as our culture deems possible? Do we, too, need to constantly second guess our interests because we heard from a talking head or a relative that we're not meeting their expectations of femininity or masculinity?

Mercifully, no. Our identity as male and female image-bearers of Christ is a solid one because it's not tied to what our culture thinks at the time. Our identity is rooted in how God made us. He made us male and female; He made us image-bearers of Him, distinctly different and unique creatures who are hardwired for unity. Unity is always God's ultimate goal, and that unity comes from our deep desire to find a supportive and loving community with our brothers and sisters in Christ—those who love us for exactly who God made us to be. But it also comes from our desire for the union of marriage. Yes, God made us intentionally male and female, and He made us to desire community and unity with others—He didn't base our identity on meeting a cultural expectation.

At the end of the day, our culture changes constantly. The rules and expectations can change so incredibly quickly, and if we're basing our identity on what our culture tells us is right, we're going to spend the rest of our lives changing to meet an ever-moving goal. Instead, we as Christ followers base our identity in Jesus. We were formed by God Himself, knit together in our mother's womb, so that we would be His image-bearers in the world and tell God's amazing story of love for His children.

More than anything, basing our worth and our identity in who God made us to be means it isn't up for debate. Our identity is and will always be as children of God, His image-bearers. We can receive and move forward in our true identity with confidence and freedom. By understanding this, we are empowered, along with our close, daily relationship and purification from Jesus Christ, to fight off temptation.

## YOU ARE MY SON

When discussing temptation, Jesus followers love to remind one another that Jesus was tempted for forty days in the desert. And this makes sense! It's a powerful story, and His time in the wilderness gives us so many powerful truths to cling to when we find ourselves being tempted. But look back a bit before Jesus begins to walk into the wilderness. Shortly before His forty-day trial, Jesus gets baptized, and in Luke 3:22 we see something amazing happen in response to Christ's baptism: "the Holy Spirit descended on him in bodily form like a dove. And a voice came from heaven: 'You are my Son, whom I love; with you I am well pleased.'"

In that moment, Jesus made a choice to begin fulfilling His calling based on knowing who He was in the Father. And God responded in kind, affirming that fact by saying, "You are my Son, whom I love; with you I am well pleased." Before Jesus ever did any public ministry or miracle, God the Father told His Son that He was pleased with Him. It was the confidence in His identity, the confidence in His Father, and the confidence in what He was called to accomplish here on Earth that gave Jesus the strength to fight off temptation those forty days in the wilderness.

Obviously, you and I are fallible. We're not always going to make the right call, and we're not always going to overcome temptation. However, it is that confidence in our identity that will not only help us overcome temptation, but it can also help us return to Christ and walk in the freedom we have in His forgiveness. It's so easy to identify ourselves by our sin and our shame, but when we do that—when we ignore the truth that we are male or female image-bearers of God—we undercut the amazing power of God's story.

More than anything, hope and identity are inextricably linked. If we believe that our identity is tied to (or cheapened by) our past failures, our weaknesses, or our sin, then it strikes the hope we find in Christ out of our worldview. If we don't see how Christ can and has redeemed us, if our story doesn't hold an unshakeable identity in Him, then we aren't moving through our lives with the knowledge of who we are meant to be. And because of that, we begin to make choices based on bad information. Thinking back to Jesus' time in the wilderness, we got to see how being affirmed and confident in His identity helped Him have the strength to withstand temptation. But as we continue to follow Jesus' time on Earth, it was the hope He had in His identity that helped Him reach out to His disciples and those He came into contact with. It's what gave Him the fortitude and love to surrender His life to die on a cross.

When you and I as Christ followers base our identity in our sin and shame, what reason do we have to resist temptation from the enemy? If, regardless of our choices, we're only going to be identified by our failures, what reason is there to try to do better? If we are permanently labeled and marred by our past, then our presence in any sort of holy story would only serve as a distraction, right? It would then make sense for us to simply give up and let the currents of life take us wherever it takes us.

However, when we step into and remain in the truth of our identity in Christ, when we stand firm in the fact that we are children of God—image-bearers of the Savior of the world—and that our sins have been washed away by Jesus' sacrifice on the cross, *everything* changes. This is the hope we're talking about that is tied to our identity. Standing in the truth that we are saved by grace and our sins have been paid for by Christ's blood means there is suddenly a point—a very important one. Instead of simply waffling along by ourselves, getting caught up in cultural currents, and trying and failing to do better on our own power, we're now an active part in God's amazing story, and as male and female image-bearers, our lives help tell His story. We can move through our lives, face temptation, and move forward in the confidence of our one true, unshakeable, unchangeable identity in Christ.

## SEXUAL STEWARDSHIP

So let's return to the first question from the start of this chapter. If our search for purity is about relationship over accomplishment, and if sex is about identity before it's about our actions, how should we move through our lives each day? Healing is what we work toward, but it's not the end of the story. Once we heal, the goal is to learn to live in freedom and forgiveness. The concept of pursuing Christ and letting Him purify us each day is great, but where do we go beyond that? The answer is sexual stewardship. It's the way you and I can look at and invest our lives, our choices, the places we spend time and money, and the content we consume. Just as we strive to be a good steward of the finances and resources given to us by God, we must also be a good steward of our sexuality and the sexual union.

It's why we've put such a fine point on constantly coming to Jesus for purification and to keep that relationship close and fruitful. The way we steward our sexuality and the sexual union is by carefully examining the choices we make, the thoughts we have, and the influences we let into our lives. And we want to be able to do that by following Jesus' teachings. When we have an intimate, close relationship with Christ, when we spend time letting Him work in our hearts, reveal His plans, and gently redirect us when we've strayed, we begin to look at the world through His eyes.

In the '90s, there was a fad where people would wear bracelets that said W.W.J.D. on them, standing for "What Would Jesus Do?" The idea behind the fad was to offer a visual reminder to Christ followers when they were faced with a tough choice so they would hopefully stop before acting and ask themselves how Jesus would respond to the situation. And though the heart of those bracelets came from a good place, it misses the point of those tough decisions we face as Christ followers. Making a so-called right decision isn't just about hypothesizing about what *we* think Jesus would do if faced with an everyday choice, such as watching a sexually explicit television show, for instance. Because ultimately, that mindset can lead to us not actively following after Christ but putting ourselves and our own thoughts, desires, and instincts before His leading.

Stewardship of anything, our sexuality included, is not about us simply guessing what Jesus would want us to do in a situation. Especially because whatever Jesus would do, He would do it perfectly and that's bad news for any of us as imperfect people. Instead, we have to remember the good news of the gospel—that it is about the relationship we have with Him—and allow Him to lead our lives and our actions. When we talk about sexual stewardship and how we can move through our lives to stay on God's path for us, thinking about how Jesus might react in a singular situation can often cause us to mistake the forest for the trees, so to speak. The actions we take, the thoughts we let steep within us, and the content we consume aren't about a series of singular choices; instead, they're about the bigger story God is telling. This is why it's so vital to remember that we are image-bearers of Christ: every single action, every single word, every single thought reflects God in some way, for better or for worse. So if we look at our lives as a series of small choices and think it's okay to stray a bit in a small area, or disregard Jesus' teaching in an area of our lives that we deem insignificant, we undercut the power and the responsibility of our identity as an image-bearer.

It goes without saying that we're not always going to make the right choice, and in this life, we'll always be walking through the cycle of sin, redemption, and purification. However, when we look at our lives as a whole—as a piece of God's amazing story of sex and the story of His love and salvation for each of us—it changes our entire perspective on our actions. When we look at our lives as image-bearers and how our actions play into God's larger story, suddenly there is more weight to our decisions. It's not about whether or not we're watching a movie or show that is too explicit, or if an artist dresses or dances a bit too provocatively. Instead, it's about stewarding our identity as image-bearers and our place in God's story.

It's for this reason that this book doesn't end with us saying, "Now you know God's better story of sex. In addition to keeping sex within the covenant of marriage, here's a list of content and activities to avoid." Because it's not up to us to tell you the places in your life that your actions or choices are distorting God's story—it's up to you to listen to Jesus as He purifies you, grows you, and leads you to choices that honor Him. Living our lives as image-bearers, understanding and being a part of God's better story of sex, isn't about labeling things as safe or unsafe, Christian or non-Christian. God's story of sex is so much better than the story we've been told, because it's not about restriction or making us seem weird in secular spaces because we haven't engaged with a piece of pop culture. It's certainly not about keeping us from having a good time. God's story of sex is so much better and life-changing for us because we're all a picture of God's love for us. Our actions, the content we consume, the things we do after we close this book aren't just about checking a box of acting in a self-described "Christian" manner (or not); it's about how we as image-bearers reflect Jesus in our actions, and how our lives and our stories weave into the larger story that's being told that points to Christ and His love and sacrifice for us.

So how are we supposed to move forward after reading this book? We understand God's better story, we've done the work on healing, and now what comes next? The stewardship part of the journey. It's the part where we each examine our lives as image-bearers and look at the things we do, the things we say, the places we go, the content we consume, and the way we interact with others and ask a vital question: how does my life reflect God and support His story? Because when we look at our lives in that manner, it means there aren't any insignificant choices—they *all* matter because our every action and mere existence are meant to be a reflection of God. And while that might seem overwhelming and like a challenge we can't meet—and you'd be right, that's why Jesus died on the cross—the great news is that we are reflections of God's better story when we follow His teaching *and* when we mess up. Because just as much as God's story is about His love for His Church and His plan to welcome us into an eternity with Him, God's story also very much acknowledges that His Church is an adulterous Bride and will mess up—frequently. It's in those moments that we get to experience the grace, love, and redemption we get when we mess up, bring our failures to the feet of Jesus, and He makes us whole again.

In short, it means that we must begin to move through our life and sexual stewardship with the knowledge of God's better story of sex, and our every action, big or small, must be judged by this one question: does this distort God's story? Does this thing distort the reflection of God in my life? If it does—be it an action, a social activity, words, songs, shows, anything—those are things that we need to take to Jesus, surrender, and allow Him to purify us and rebuild us in a way that better reflects Him.

Of course, that doesn't mean we're called to do this alone. Obviously, your personal relationship with Jesus is between you and Him, and there are aspects of personal responsibility you need to take that can range from owning up to and asking forgiveness for past mistakes or installing personal boundaries such as internet browser blockers. It doesn't mean we are to embark on stewarding our sexuality, the sexual union, and our lifelong journey as image-bearers in God's story alone. As we've said before, we're called to live in community. The protection a person gets when they are a part of an authentic community of Christ followers is vital! When it comes to sexual stewardship, that means you can lean on your community as another means to help keep you focused on your identity as an image-bearer of God and your place in God's story of sex. Your community can help keep you accountable in areas where you repeatedly fight temptation, they can call you out when you make choices that might be distorting God's story, and they can walk with you and share in that journey of constant purification through Jesus Christ.

Our lives are meant to tell a story, and our existence is meant to point to Christ. So if we can reframe the focus of our life to be on how we can best point those around us to God in our actions and our everyday life rather than what we think we can or cannot get away with, we can begin to fully experience the amazing story God is telling through our lives, and we can start seeing that story play out in the lives of those around us!

# CHAPTER 12

# SHINE YOUR LIGHT

## JOSH

We've gone on quite the journey together in the pages of this book, and hopefully it has not only started you on the journey of fully understanding and accepting God's better story of purity and sex but has also kicked off your journey of healing and restoration with Christ. While this is all good and important work, you might wonder where exactly you're supposed to go from here. Once you've begun the process of dealing with your own past and aligning yourself more with the beautiful story God is telling, what does that mean for the rest of your life? How does this knowledge of God's story of sex impact your life after reading this book? How does it impact your family? Your friends? Your church? Your community?

When we started this book, we talked about imagining a world free from sexual brokenness. Our prayer is that this freedom wouldn't just be a figment of your imagination that will always be out of reach, but that you would be able to fully understand who you are in Christ and what it means to walk in freedom. By prayerfully committing your ways to Jesus, He can begin to rebuild you and those you love right now! Your life as an image-bearer tells God's story, and it is meant to point directly to Him. This is true for all aspects of your life, so the way you engage with God's story of sex is no exception.

Both our culture and our churches have perpetuated various lies and distortion of truth that have taken God's intention for sex and the sexual union and twisted it. Some communities (faith based or otherwise) have distorted that story to such a degree that it's not even recognizable, while others have twisted it just enough to leave the subject out of focus just enough to cause confusion, fear, and shame. That's why it's vital for you and me to know, understand, and embrace God's better story in our lives, as well as share it with others.

This story God is telling, the plans He has for two image-bearers to come together, and the way He uses that beautiful and powerful union to communicate the reality of His perfect plan to be united with His creation are too good to keep to ourselves. So it's not surprising that the enemy hates the power behind God's story of sex, and it's why he has worked overtime not only to distort our understanding of God's intentions for sex and the sexual union but also to turn that story into something that Christ followers are often too embarrassed to talk about in an appropriate church setting.

Now that you understand God's better story of sex and you've seen the powerful way it can work in your life and change the way you look at yourself, your partner or spouse, and the entire purpose of the sexual union, we want to encourage you to talk about this with those in your community and those you might be leading or mentoring (again, when appropriate). God didn't give us this better story just to keep it to ourselves but to share with others! If His plans for sexuality, romantic relationships, and the sexual union are meant to help us understand His love for His children, we shouldn't want to keep it to ourselves. Additionally, talking about God's better story of sex doesn't just help clear up harmful misconceptions, but it's also how we as a body of believers can support one another and lift one another up. If we understand God's story and how it has played out in the life of a member of our community, we will better know how to pray for that person, how to support them, how to encourage them, and how to hold them accountable. Remember, we are all called to live in community with one another, and that protection and support we have from our brothers and sisters in Christ are vital to our growth as Jesus followers.

When we encourage you to talk with others about God's better story of sex, we're not saying you need to become the weirdo in your church constantly trying to initiate awkward and often wildly inappropriate conversations. No, when we say this is a story that we need to share, it means we need to share God's better story of sex with those in our close circles. Talking about sex, sexual brokenness, and the pain caused by our actions, the actions of others, and harmful teaching is a really vulnerable conversation, so these conversations need to happen in safe spaces. However, as we said, a world free from sexual brokenness starts with you and it starts with me, so it's up to us to create those safe spaces with those closest to us to share this beautiful story. We need to point those in our community to the true purity we find in a relationship with Jesus so they, too, can start their own journey of healing and restoration.

The reality is, our culture is screaming their narrative on sex. We see it everywhere in songs, movies, shows, even advertisements. So if we keep God's amazing story of sex quiet because we feel uncomfortable, it's going to get utterly lost in the cacophonous waves of misinformation coming from our culture. However, on the other hand, in response to our culture's perspective on sex, the church has historically overcorrected, and the fruit of that overcorrection is the purity culture.

Worse yet, in our attempt to overcorrect cultural input, we've turned a mere conversation surrounding sex and the sexual union into a dirty, inappropriate, or shameful thing, and many communities of believers have spun the narrative that simply suppressing the conversation around sex will somehow help a person in their pursuit of purity. But that's not what God wants! Obviously, there is a time and a place for everything, and not every story is appropriate for every audience. However, God never meant for us to be ashamed to talk about sex, nor did He intend for us to suppress the discussion of it to help us save ourselves and our purity. God talks about sex and the sexual union a lot in the Bible! He repeatedly refers to His Church as His Bride, and Himself as the Bridegroom! He refers to our ultimate unity in heaven with Him as a wedding celebration and the consummation of the ages! God wasn't ashamed of His story. He boldly proclaimed it throughout the Bible.

Isaiah 43:19 says, "See, I am doing a new thing! Now it springs up; do you not perceive it? I am making a way in the wilderness and streams in the wasteland." That verse is the perfect picture of how God's story of sex and His love for His Church are meant to be something so much better, so much more powerful, and so different from the message our culture teaches us. If you've read through this book and thought, *Wow, God's story of sex feels so different from everything I've heard about sex on television,* or even, *God's story of sex feels so different from all of those youth group meetings that left me scared and embarrassed as a teen,* it's because His story *is* so different. He's doing something amazing, beautiful, and life-changing, and it's up to you and me to boldly share it with our communities.

We have the better story, so we need to proclaim it boldly and intentionally, which means we need to capitalize on the opportune moments God puts in our path. God will ordain those moments. Remember the story we shared earlier about the thirteen-year-old-girl who talked about being raped at eight years old and how we were able to shut down the harmful teachings she received from her church that told her she was broken and her purity had been forever stolen from her? God put a moment in my (Dan's) path, and I had the choice either to share God's better story boldly and intentionally or get uncomfortable and walk away while leaving that little girl in the heartache and hopelessness she began her day with. It's up to you and me to ask probing questions of those in our community. It's up to us to confess to our community when we miss the mark. It's up to us to make time with those closest to us—especially if we have kids or a young person in our lives whom we're helping to raise—and start this conversation. From there, we can initiate this conversation in our churches, which will lead to teaching, engagement, healing, and growth around sex and sexual issues. Doing this can feel uncomfortable at first, but it's a vital process to start in our communities, because every time we choose to stay silent about sex (or any important topic, for that matter), we're allowing our culture around us to have the more prominent voice. Whether we like it or not, the world is going to speak about sex, which means our job is to speak even louder!

## WHO MADE MAN'S MOUTH?

Of course, it would be naïve to think that the only reason a person might be hesitant to have an open, honest, and vulnerable conversation about sex is due to the potential awkwardness. Talking about sex gets to the core of our personhood and talking about it plainly can make us feel incredibly exposed. Asking questions about sex, confessing our own brokenness, sharing fears, or sharing past trauma is a wildly vulnerable thing to do because it exposes things we have been so good at hiding. It's easy to look at those parts of your life and your unique brand of brokenness and think, *Well, I'm willing to accept that Jesus can forgive me and make me new, but I'm probably a bit too broken to minister to other people. I should leave this to someone with a better past.*

But here's the real truth: the fear and shame we feel when we keep our brokenness a secret is an incredibly effective tool of the enemy. When we allow fear to keep us from being vulnerable, we are closing ourselves off and never fully letting another person in to see who we really are and the work Christ is doing in us. Remember, the Bible doesn't just refer to the Church as the Bride of Christ. We're also referred to as the adulterous Bride, which means that God fully knows and expects that we are going to mess up, that we are absolutely broken, and that we all are in desperate need of Christ and His redemption. Our brokenness and the way Jesus saved us and purifies us is an integral part of God's better story of sex. So the last thing we should do is discount ourselves or say that we aren't the right person to talk about this stuff because of our past.

The Bible has a great example of someone who tried to slide out of God's path for him. When God appeared to Moses in the form of a burning bush, telling him to confront Pharaoh to let the Israelites go, Moses got uncomfortable. He felt incredibly unsure about stepping into such an important role, and he even said he wasn't good at speaking, so he'd be a bad person to be a mouthpiece for God. Some people have thought the reason was because Moses was uncomfortable with public speaking or because he had a stutter or other speech impediment, or both. But regardless of why Moses felt ill-equipped, when God said He had a plan for Moses, watch how he responded: "Pardon your servant, Lord. I have never been eloquent, neither in the past nor since you have spoken to your servant. I am slow of speech and tongue" (Exodus 4:10).

Instead of God saying something like, "Oh, thanks for telling Me. I'll find someone else who's a great public speaker! Thanks, Moses!" God responded to him in verses 11–12 with this powerful truth: "Who gave human beings their mouths? Who makes them deaf or mute? Who gives them sight or makes them blind? Is it not I, the Lord? Now go; I will help you speak and will teach you what to say."

It's a powerful reminder to you and me. When God has a plan for us, when He sends us out to speak on His behalf, the reason is not about us or our ability to eloquently speak to a crowd; it's not about our social media platform; and it's not about us having a picture-perfect story that covers the details of our sin. God is calling you and He is calling me—just as we are, right now. He wants to use *all* of our stories and the powerful ways He has worked in our lives to point us back to Him and His goodness. When we try to duck out of that calling because of our fear and shame, when we fall prey to that tactic from the enemy, we're inadvertently standing in the way of how Christ wants to heal and redeem our communities. Obviously, our inaction isn't going to stop Christ from showing up, but we will definitely miss out on the exciting opportunities God presents to us to be used to point to His glory.

As a dad, I (Josh) got my world completely rocked when I first learned about pureHOPE and the ministry's message back in 2010. After learning about God's better story of sex and reframing the idea of purity to a relationship, I was in constant prayer, asking for a door to open for me to share this with my son. That door opened when a close friend had a miscarriage. My son came to me and asked how our friends would ever have another baby after losing one, and I saw very clearly that the Lord had opened the door to start the conversation about sex. And what followed was about an hour of discussing God's intention for sex and how His intention for that union was far better than anything purity culture or mainstream culture tried to teach. The conversation wasn't perfect, and I'm sure I didn't say all of the right things, but I was open to Christ's leading, and I answered the call when He led me to be vulnerable and speak. All I did was show up and be willing. God used that opportune moment and gave me the words to share this important truth with my son that so often we, as parents, feel too uncomfortable to broach. I'm happy to say that the openness of that conversation was the beginning of a dialogue that kept the door open for him to come to me with concerns and questions that came up as he grew older. It has made our relationship incredibly open and honest. Don't get me wrong, right now my son is sixteen, so things aren't always rosy and perfect between us, but that conversation all of those years ago laid an important foundation in my relationship with my son as he has grown.

This is why we need to be open to those authentic conversations, whether they happen with our kids, friends, family, or spouse. When we are open to God's leading and are honest about ourselves with others when we talk about God's intentions for sex, amazing things can happen. When we stop being fake, when we stop trying to maintain the image of being a "perfect Christian," and when we reject the idea that sex is dirty and something a nice Christian doesn't talk about, we can show our true hearts and our authentic selves to another person. And that's a powerful thing.

So when it comes to talking about God's better story of sex, it also means we need to intentionally make spaces where we can be real and be vulnerable. It also means owning up to our mistakes and fully confessing to God. This doesn't mean giving a graphic play-by-play of every instance of our sin, but rather breaking through those boundaries of fear and shame and owning up to past (or present) messes because we strayed beyond the guardrails God put up for us. Part of experiencing freedom from sexual bro-kenness also means experiencing freedom from the fear and shame we've carried from our mistakes or from those who have grossly misguided us. So when we are vulnerable and fully confess our sins or confide in someone about past trauma, when we honestly share questions or concerns, we can find support from that person and healing from God. We can step out of the cage that fear and shame have kept us locked in.

In turn, not only are we free, but those in our community are encour-aged to seek freedom too. The forgiveness, redemption, and restoration others see in us will hopefully cause them to seek that same forgiveness and freedom in Him. When we can be open and show that part of our lives to our community, it points directly to our Savior and what purity is really about—that dynamic relationship with Christ and His daily work in our lives to make us new.

As we said, vulnerability can often come in the form of confession, but it can also be about letting someone else into the hidden parts of your heart. You can let someone in on questions, concerns, or fears you might have. You might be wrestling through something you heard or were told. Or maybe you're processing through trauma. Either way, when you come to someone and let them in by saying something as innocuous as, "Hey, can we talk about something I'm struggling with?" or maybe even, "I see you're walking through something I went through myself, and if you're interested, I'd like to help you avoid some of my mistakes." Doing this invites the other person to enter into your personal space, which is key. Being open and vulnerable about our weak points, trauma, and broken-ness is vital for creating the environment needed for spreading the truth of God's story of sex.

## I'VE BEEN THERE

If you need to talk to someone right now about a really intense issue or a very sensitive problem you are going through, who would you go to? What if that problem painted you in a negative light? Would that person change toward you? What if the issue was something really delicate to discuss or potentially awkward? Would you still go to that same person? Do you have someone who instantly popped into your head? Or are you struggling to name someone? Don't freak out if that is the case, because a lot of us find ourselves in that boat, especially when it comes to sex. And while you might still need to seek out who that person could be in your own life, the best news about the knowledge you've gained in this book and the healing journey you've begun to embark on with Christ is that you can now be that person for someone else.

If you've spent any time in the church, you won't be surprised to hear that there aren't a ton of great places to go if you've got questions, concerns, fears, or struggles about sex. It's why we oftentimes end up looking in secular spaces to find a truly safe person. But the problem with that is, there is often a fundamental disconnect since the basic worldviews don't match up. Embracing the secular worldview is the quickest way for distortions of God's story of sex to get spread around faith-based communities. However, when you and I become more vulnerable about what is going on in our hearts and our minds when it comes to sex, we make ourselves that safe space for someone else (or even several other people). When we are honest about our struggles, it not only gives permission for those in our community to be honest with us as well, but it also likely sends one of the most important messages out to someone: you're not alone.

Knowing that those secretive parts of yourself—those things you're so embarrassed or ashamed about that you can't even bring yourself to write them down in a journal—are things that others have wrestled with too is vital when it comes to healing. When someone hears you express a struggle you've also wrestled with, and you are honest about some of the ugliest, most shameful parts of that struggle, it offers such a feeling of hope. When you can say, "Oh yeah, I've struggled with that exact same thing, and here's what Jesus did for me," it throws open the curtains and finally lets light spill in to fill the darkest corners of another struggling person's heart.

There is freedom and life that come from confession and shining light on those dark parts of our hearts. When we allow our brokenness to hide in the darkness, it festers and grows and can wreak utter havoc on us. Think about it this way: If you spotted mold growing in your basement and thought, *Yikes, that's not good! But it's embarrassing to admit I've got a mold problem, so I'll just block off the basement and keep it dark so I can't see it,* it wouldn't take long for your basement to be absolutely gnarly—even dangerous—due to the out-of-control mold problem. The same thing happens within our hearts when we keep our brokenness, sin, and shame in the dark.

First John 1:5–7 says this about bringing our sin into the light: "This is the message we have heard from him and declare to you: God is light; in him there is no darkness at all. If we claim to have fellowship with him and yet walk in the darkness, we lie and do not live out the truth. But if we walk in the light, as he is in the light, we have fellowship with one another, and the blood of Jesus, his Son, purifies us from all sin." As Christ followers, we are hardwired toward confession. It's how we pursue purification in our relationship with Jesus, and it's how we build community. Every time we bring those areas of shame or brokenness into the light through confession, that sin loses some of its power over us. Even better, it opens the door for others in our community to open up as well.

When you are open about your sin and the areas you struggle, the brothers and sisters in Christ that you walk through life with get to hear your heart in a real and vulnerable way. They will suddenly realize that they aren't the only one who struggles. It's such a vital piece to building authentic community because vulnerability shown through confession and honest discussions about sin and struggle opens the door to creating a safe space for others to say, "Oh, yes, exactly. Me too. I'm dealing with that too." The moment this happens, sin doesn't just lose its power over the person confessing, it also loses its power over those listening and are now able to speak their truth as well. The times I've felt the freedom to confess any of my struggles to a trusted friend or mentor, I was met with grace and understanding. It's such a feeling of love and freedom to show someone else the thing you're ashamed of, and to see them embody the love and grace of our Savior by walking alongside you as you repent and heal from that sin.

Likewise, it is an incredible gift to be that friend or mentor to someone who is confessing their struggles to you. It's amazing to hear someone tell you, either in explicit terms or in a general sense because of their actions, that they feel safe enough around you to be vulnerable and expose an area of intense struggle. It can feel really tempting to bring your sin and struggles to Christ and decide that from there you'll deal with the repercussions of your brokenness on your own, so you don't disappoint or burden those around you. But being open about the parts of your story that are broken is one of the most beautiful things about being a part of the body of Christ, and Jesus uses those times when you and I choose to be vulnerable about our struggles not only to heal and minister to the person confessing, but to heal and minister to those listening. And we miss out on that when we choose to stay silent because of our fear or shame.

It's exactly the same when it comes to talking about struggles with sex. We've conditioned ourselves to simply "keep what happens in the bedroom in the bedroom." However, that secrecy will eat you alive. Whether you're struggling with a sexual relationship outside of marriage, you're consuming harmful content, you're fighting against thoughts that you know go against God's teaching, or you're trying to figure out why you and your spouse are having a tough time with sex even though you waited until marriage, if we don't have any place we can go to talk it out, the enemy has more than enough tools to whip up the fear and shame machine to trap us. What might start as an errant thought of, *Oh, we'll figure this out. I don't need to bother anyone with this,* can soon balloon into a huge monstrous mountain that keeps us putting up barrier after barrier because we think we're too broken, too sick, too disgusting, too weird, too damaged…

When we can become that person others know they can come to with questions, concerns, and struggles about sex, we not only get a clear avenue to share and discuss God's better story of sex, but we also get to extend a hand to our brothers and sisters in Christ and say, "You're not alone. I've been there too."

First Peter 2:9 says, "But you are a chosen people, a royal priesthood, a holy nation, God's special possession, that you may declare the praises of him who called you out of darkness into his wonderful light." We're designed as followers of Christ to be open about the ways Christ redeemed us and how He called us out of our darkness into His wonderful light. It's part of God's basic design for humanity, and when we can make ourselves vulnerable and become the person our community knows will listen when it comes to questions or struggles regarding sex without condemnation, we're falling right into step with God's plan for His Church and His story. More than that, we get to extend a hand and invite that person on the journey with us. We can link arms with them and embark on the journey to pursue Christ and experience daily purification from Him together.

# EPILOGUE

## LOOKING TO THE FUTURE

As you finish up this book, we hope that you'll turn the last page finally understanding God's better story of sex. We hope you'll be encouraged that His story and His plans are far better for us than anything we've been told, and that it doesn't matter where our past took us and how horribly we've messed up. Our purity isn't something we were in charge of in the first place—we never were. No one is damaged goods, and our purity can't be lost. When Christ paid the price for us on the cross, He redeemed us, and we get to spend the rest of our time on Earth pursuing a relationship with Him as He purifies us. It's not our job to save ourselves—it will never be our job to do that. And when it comes to looking at our lives, our choices, and the rules we follow when it comes to sex, we hope that you can see them as the guardrails for safety, not as killjoys. When you look at those areas of your life, you can now see it's not about what the right thing to do is or the Christian thing to do, but what is helping tell God's story of sex and what is distorting it. We hope this book has helped you refocus your life as something, sex notwithstanding, that is meant to always point directly to Christ.

None of us always gets this right, but we serve a God who forgives and we have a Savior who redeems and restores. Because of this, we can move forward with confidence knowing that our identity as a child of God is secure, our purity is in Christ's hands, and that He can even work that our shortcomings into a way that points to Him. We just have to be open to His redirection while looking for ways to share this amazing story to our community.

Our prayer for you is that you will not only allow Christ to do His healing work in you as you work to understand and follow His guidelines for His better story of sex, but that you will begin paying attention to His prompting when you are presented with those situations, opportunities, and encounters where you can talk about His better story.

# ACKNOWLEDGMENTS

To Dr. Jerry Kirk, whose love for God and heart for His people led him to leave his pastoral role and found the ministry of pureHOPE in 1983. Jerry's life and ministry continue to influence many and we honor his faithfulness and courage that cleared a path for us to do this great work.

The late Rick Schatz, who fearlessly paved the way to bring the message of pureHOPE to a generation hungry for a better narrative. Rick provided organizational structure, and his love for the ministry was felt by everyone who benefited from knowing him.

The late Jack Samad was instrumental in opening the eyes of Christian parents and leaders to the coming tsunami of technological advances that would impact the lives of everyone. Jack coupled his love of God's people with creative talent to tell a better story through media.

To our brother, friend, and partner in ministry Noel Bouché. Thank you for being a leader we trust, honor, and respect. Your many years of leadership and vision casting continue to guide and direct our ministry's work and mission. We could not have written this book without your vision, guidance, and inspiration. Thank you, Noel, for your commitment to excellence, your passion for Jesus, and for throwing us the ball. Love you, bro!

To our current President and ministry leader, Jasper Hall. Where do we begin? Your poise and calm demeanor are a comfort to everyone who interacts with you. You have done a stellar job filling some big shoes, and your imprint on this ministry is already being noticed. Thank you for giving us the freedom to dream big and go wherever the Lord is leading. We love you, Nesper!

This book would not be possible without the dedicated work of our dear friend and ministry advocate, Aszia Pearson. She has worked tirelessly to create life-changing resources that have been consumed by people all around the world and have faithfully proclaimed God's better story of sex for over a decade. Thank you, Aszia, for inspiring everyone you encounter to engage with truth, experience freedom, and live out of an overflow of hope.

To the rest of our pureHOPE team. Your hard work and dedication don't go unnoticed. Much like the body of Christ, each one of you plays a significant role in this ministry's impact and we couldn't touch lives around the world without your commitment and dedication. You are called for such a time as this and we love each one of you! We are family!

We don't deserve the grace extended to us by our friends at the Fedd Agency. Thank you for putting up with our constant video calls and emails when we had no idea what we were doing. Thank you for believing in us and are blessed to have worked with you.

To our dear friend, Kendall Davis. Over a year ago, you knew nothing about pureHOPE, but you've been able to take loads of content and bring simplicity and clarity. Thank you for your hard work in helping us bring this book to life.

To our many faithful supporters. We are grateful for your investment both big and small. Your generosity has allowed us to create world-class content that reaches thousands of people around the world. Thank you for believing in what we do, and we pray the Lord's richest blessings on you.

Most importantly, to our Savior, our Healer, our Redeemer, and our soon-coming King. You are the greatest Author, the One who writes the greatest stories. Thank you for trusting us with the responsibility of sharing your truth. We are honored and humbled! Thank you for salvation! Thank you for your forgiveness. Thank you for setting the captives free. Thank you that you are the Author and Finisher of our faith. Thank you that your mercies are new every morning. Thank you that when we are weak, you are strong. We are nothing without you, so we thank you for the Holy Spirit that guides us each day. Thank you for calling us out of darkness into your marvelous light. Thank you for peace that passes understanding and that all our hope is found in you. May your name be praised to the ends of the earth.

# ADDITIONAL RESOURCES

To check out our speaking schedule, to reach out to our team, or to explore the other books and resources we have available, go to our website: purehope.net.

If you or someone you know has been the victim of sexual assault, you can consult the National Sexual Assault Hotline at 1-800-656-4673. The line is open twenty-four hours a day, seven days a week. You can also chat with someone online twenty-four hours a day at online.rainn.org.

If you, or someone you know, need help against human trafficking, the National Human Trafficking Hotline is 1-888-373-7888. You can also text HELP or INFO to 233733, or head to their website: humantraffickinghotline.org.

# ENDNOTES

1  "New Marriage and Divorce Statistics Released," Barna Group, accessed April 13, 2021, https://www.barna.com/research/new-marriage-and-divorce-statistics-released/.

2  "What's the Average Age of a Child's First Exposure to Porn?" Fight the New Drug, November 24, 2020, https://fightthenewdrug.org/real-average-age-of-first-exposure/.

3  Louie, Sam. "Sexual Behaviors in Children," Psychology Today, Sussex Publishers, April 24, 2019, https://www.psychologytoday.com/us/blog/minority-report/201904/sexual-behaviors-in-children.

4  "2019 U.S. National Human Trafficking Hotline Statistics," Polaris, November 12, 2020, https://polarisproject.org/2019-us-national-human-trafficking-hotline-statistics/.

5  See note 3.